THE HAMLYN LECTURES

ELEVENTH SERIES

JUDGE AND JURIST IN THE REIGN OF VICTORIA

AUSTRALIA
The Law Book Co. of Australasia Pty Ltd.
Sydney : Melbourne : Brisbane

CANADA AND U.S.A.
The Carswell Company Ltd.
Toronto

INDIA
N. M. Tripathi Private Ltd.
Bombay

NEW ZEALAND
Sweet & Maxwell (N.Z.) Ltd.
Wellington

PAKISTAN
Pakistan Law House
Karachi

JUDGE AND JURIST

IN THE

REIGN OF VICTORIA

BY

C. H. S. FIFOOT, M.A., F.B.A.

of the Middle Temple, Barrister-at-Law,
Reader in Common Law to the Council
of Legal Education

Published under the auspices of
THE HAMLYN TRUST

LONDON
STEVENS AND SONS LIMITED
1959

*First published in 1959 by
Stevens & Sons Limited
of 11 New Fetter Lane
London — Law Publishers
and printed in Great Britain
by The Eastern Press Ltd.
of London and Reading*

CONTENTS

HAMLYN LECTURERS

1949   The Right Hon. Lord Denning

1950   Richard O'Sullivan, Q.C.

1951   F. H. Lawson, D.C.L.

1952   A. L. Goodhart, K.B.E., Q.C., F.B.A.

1953   Sir Carleton Kemp Allen, Q.C., F.B.A.

1954   C. J. Hamson, M.A., LL.M.

1955   Glanville Williams, LL.D.

1956   The Hon. Sir Patrick Devlin

1957   The Right Hon. Lord MacDermott

1958   Sir David Hughes Parry, Q.C., M.A., LL.D., D.C.L.

1959   C. H. S. Fifoot, M.A., F.B.A.

THE HAMLYN TRUST

THE Hamlyn Trust came into existence under the will of the late Miss Emma Warburton Hamlyn, of Torquay, who died in 1941, aged eighty. She came of an old and well-known Devon family. Her father, William Bussell Hamlyn, practised in Torquay as a solicitor for many years. She was a woman of dominant character, intelligent and cultured, well versed in literature, music and art, and a lover of her country. She inherited a taste for law, and studied the subject. She travelled frequently on the Continent and about the Mediterranean and gathered impressions of comparative jurisprudence and ethnology.

Miss Hamlyn bequeathed the residue of her estate in terms which were thought vague. The matter was taken to the Chancery Division of the High Court, which on November 29, 1948, approved a scheme for the administration of the Trust. Paragraph 3 of the Scheme is as follows:

" The object of this charity is the furtherance by lectures or otherwise among the Common People of the United Kingdom of Great Britain and Northern Ireland of the knowledge of the Comparative Jurisprudence and the Ethnology of the chief European countries, including the United Kingdom, and the circumstances of the growth of such jurisprudence to the intent that the Common People of the United Kingdom may realise the privileges which in law and custom they enjoy in

CHAPTER 1

1837–1901 : JUDGE AND JURIST

QUEEN VICTORIA was not born a Victorian : she became one by marriage, widowhood and longevity. Upon the crowded years of her reign no single pattern may be imposed. A few contrasts will mark the gulf between 1837 and 1901. In 1837 Sir Walter Scott was but five years dead, Carlyle published his *French Revolution*, *Pickwick Papers* were appearing in numbers, Disraeli entered the House of Commons for the first time. In 1901 Thomas Hardy had ceased to write novels, Henry James had reached the last stage of refinement, Bernard Shaw had surrendered dramatic criticism to the incomparable Max and was meditating upon Man and Superman, Winston Churchill had been a year in Parliament. Today's observer, looking back upon the reign with his own resigned, almost cynical assumption of instability, may see it enveloped in an atmosphere of smug security. The impression is superficial. From 1837 to 1850 England was, or felt itself to be, in constant peril of revolution. These were the years of Corn Law agitation, of the Chartists, of mob disorder, of the reverberations at home of 1848 abroad. They saw the advent of the railway and the company, with their deep impact upon the structure of trade and industry, the first erosion of individual responsibility and the gradual disintegration of provincial life.

If any period invites the reproach of complacency,

it is the third quarter of the century. The Great
Exhibition of 1851 symbolised the supremacy of the
upper middle class—able, confident, high-minded,
broad based upon commercial and agricultural wealth.
They and their sons were the fruits of the new public
schools inspired by Dr. Arnold, who had taught them
the importance of being earnest. Their leader was
Lord Palmerston, born above them but adopted into
their *familia* and, in the cliché of the time, a repre-
sentative man. His death in October, 1865, still in
office and within two days of his eighty-first birthday,
was a climacteric. The rivals who sought his place,
Gladstone and Disraeli, came from the dominant
class, but new men meant new measures. The Reform
Act of 1867, if it seemed apt to buttress the structure
of society, could serve as well to undermine it. Beneath
the surface of popular optimism and material prosperity
lurked the fear of the future. Thinking men searched
their minds and were perturbed at what they found.
Anthony Trollope, the mirror of his age and class,
portrayed with distaste the transition from the old
England of *The Warden* in 1855 to the new England
of *Mr. Scarborough's Family* in 1882. Froude in
1864 was prophetic. " We live in times of disintegration,
and none can tell what will be after us. What opinions
—what convictions—the infant of today will find
prevailing on the earth if he and it live out together
to the middle of another century, only a bold man
would undertake to conjecture." [1] The testimony of
Bagehot, shrewd and detached, is significant. He had

[1] *The Science of History*, a lecture delivered on Feb. 5, 1864,
and included in *Short Studies*, I, 32.

been bred to assume the merits of the current " system of removable inequalities " much as, in a later age, it has become orthodox to assert, rather than to rationalise, the cruder doctrine of equality. It was " the wholesome competition between class and class and the wholesome migration from class to class " that forged " the strongest instruments of social improvement." This assumption he now saw challenged by the advent of democracy —" neither the best nor the highest form which a society can adopt, and one fatal to that development of individual originality by which the past progress of the human race has been achieved and from which alone all future progress is to be anticipated." [2]

The prophets were justified only too soon. In the last quarter of the century powerful solvents were at work upon English society. The agricultural interests, which had so surprisingly survived and even flourished upon the abolition of the Corn Laws, fell into a decline that proved all but fatal. International competition, inherent in the dogma of Free Trade, at last burst the barriers of insularity, and the produce of the new acres was carried by the new means of transport to flood the domestic markets. In this invasion high and low—landlord, farmer and labourer—were alike engulfed.[3] From the late seventies to the early nineties

---

[2] *Literary Studies*, II, 124–126. Bagehot here chastises Thackeray for chastising snobs. In the second edition of his *English Constitution* (1872) he expressed his fear " of the ignorant multitude " enfranchised by the Reform Act.

[3] The results of the agricultural collapse were marked in remote places. " An income which [in 1875] was little short of £1,100 is now [1883], through the fall in agricultural prices, not more than £750 " (*Adventures of Sherlock Holmes, The Speckled Band*).

agricultural was accompanied by trade depression, with its familiar portents—unemployment, strikes, the foundation of the Fabian Society and the rise of the Labour Party. Amid this confusion political and economic *laissez-faire*, long fashionable if never unquestioned, could not survive unimpaired ; and the reactions of anxious Liberals to the new machinery of state control were, according to temperament, tortuous or indignant. Some, like T. H. Green, vindicated the measures of their leaders by insisting that only through order could freedom be realised. Defending the Employers' Liability Act of 1880 against the reproach of authoritarianism, he insisted that contractual licence was " valuable only as a means to an end—the liberation of the powers of all men equally for contribution to the common good." [4] Liberty must serve equality. Herbert Spencer, fed on the pure milk of individualism, was not to be comforted by paradox. The servant could too easily become the slave. In 1884 in *The Man versus the State* he vented his anguish at the betrayal of liberal ideas and denounced the " trend towards regimentation, bureaucracy, socialism and excessive taxation." [5] Victoria's reign, with its material achievements and its accumulation of wealth, ended, as it had begun, in doubt and misgiving.

Through all these years educated opinion was moulded by a diversity of intellectual interests. The young Victorian inherited the economic theories of

---

[4] *Liberal Legislation and Freedom of Contract* (1881), in his *Collected Works*, 365.

[5] See in *The Man versus the State* the essay entitled " The Coming Slavery."

Ricardo, modified and disseminated by John Stuart Mill, whose *Principles of Political Economy*, published in 1847, was in 1901 still the one " set book " on economics in the Oxford History School. By this time, indeed, its premises were widely challenged, nor had they ever lacked critics. Carlyle had rejected them with scorn. Mill's book, he said, was " well done but not worth doing." But they helped to form the climate in which were bred most of the judges and jurists of Victoria's reign.[6]

A fresh and stimulating demand upon receptive minds was made by natural science and pre-eminently by the biologist. Opinion was excited in 1844 by the anonymous publication of *Vestiges of the Natural Order of Creation*, attributed *inter alios* to the Prince Consort but in fact written by Robert Chambers of *Chambers's Encyclopaedia*. It popularised " evolution " and was eagerly embraced and as furiously denounced.[7] The way was prepared for Darwin, whose theory of natural selection met so happily the claims of a competitive society ; and in 1869 Bagehot applied biological methods to sociology.[8]

[6] Mr. Justice Byles was a distinguished exception. He wrote in 1849 a trenchant book on *The Sophisms of Free Trade*, which went through eight editions. But he was in everything a conservative. He rode to the courts on an aged white horse ; and, in honour of his work on *Bills of Exchange*, was saluted with cries of " Here comes Byles on Bills ! "

[7] It was parodied by Disraeli in *Tancred*. " It explains everything," said Lady Constance. " First there was nothing, then there was something ; then, I forget the next, I think there were shells, then fishes. Then we came. And the next stage will be something very superior to us, something with wings. . . . This is development. We had fins : we may have wings."

[8] *Physics and Politics*.

The bias thus imparted to speculative thought seemed to threaten the foundations of religious belief. Newman, as he avowed in his *Apologia*, felt instantly the danger to Christian faith, or at least to Christian doctrine, of scientific pretensions; and the appearance in 1860 of the famous *Essays and Reviews* revealed the need felt by the more sensitive leaders of the Anglican Church to trim their lamps to the new revelation. Of the seven contributors Benjamin Jowett, Mark Pattison and Frederick Temple were at once the most distinguished and the most circumspect. Two of their colleagues, more enthusiastic or less discreet, were prosecuted before the Court of Arches for denying the doctrine of eternal punishment. They were convicted, but the conviction was quashed by the Judicial Committee of the Privy Council. The fortunate ambiguity of the Articles enabled the charge of heresy to be eluded. Lord Westbury, who delivered the opinion of the Committee, was said, in a contemporary squib, to have " dismissed Hell with costs and to have taken away from members of the Church of England their last hope of everlasting damnation." [9] Outside the ranks of the clergy belief sank only too often into agnosticism. The loss of faith was a catastrophe in itself enough to destroy the picture of a nation engrossed in creature comfort. The best suffered the most. Stable standards of conduct must somewhere be found, and with doubtful hope the religious was replaced by the ethical imperative. George Eliot, while she felt it difficult, if not impossible, to accept orthodox Christianity, was not comforted by the prospect of evolution.

[9] See Geoffrey Faber's *Jowett*, Chaps. 11 and 12.

After reading the *Origin of Species* she wrote : " To me the Development Theory, and all other explanations of processes by which things came to be, produce a feeble impression compared with the mystery that lies under the processes." [10] Matthew Arnold, loth to relinquish all conception of a Deity, could describe God only as " the Eternal not ourselves which makes for righteousness." Bradley's comment is not unjust. As well term the habit of washing " the Eternal not ourselves that makes for cleanliness." [11]

A healthier phenomenon was the emergence from Germany of the " historical spirit." Niebuhr, Savigny and above all Ranke may be called the founders of modern history. They proclaimed the need to base all research and all writing upon the study of original sources ; and when in 1870 Stubbs published his *Select Charters* he vindicated at once German technique and English scholarship. The influence of Germany was not confined to history. It flowed through every branch of English culture. As early as 1792 in Edinburgh a coterie of briefless barristers, among them Walter Scott, formed a German class. The example spread southwards until Coleridge and Carlyle became ardent disciples. English philosophers followed at the heels of Kant and deserted him in the second half of the century only to cultivate the more esoteric rites of Hegel. Theologians, willingly or grudgingly, went again to school. Pusey himself served an apprenticeship with the German divines, though he was proof against the scepticism with which his younger

[10] Cross, *Life of George Eliot*, II, 148.
[11] F. H. Bradley, *Ethical Studies*, 283.

contemporaries were infected. Dean Stanley defended
Essays and Reviews by invoking the testimony of the
master race. " The German theologians have lighted
the candle which, by God's grace, shall never be put
out." [12]

English law was not insulated from these currents
of thought and opinion. Ethical preoccupations
coloured the approach to civil and criminal liability.[13]
The prevalent political economy demanded, as one of
its assumptions, the sanctity of agreements, and it
was in the first half of Victoria's reign that the classical
formulae of contract were expounded. Expanding
trade and industry, with their prolific and costly litigation, drew to the common law and to the commercial
bar the eager minds that had previously pursued the
mysteries of conveyancing.[14]

The literature of the law reflected the taste for
biological investigation. Maine published his *Ancient
Law* two years after the *Origin of Species*, and it was
the theory of natural selection no less than a sense of
the past that provoked his attack on Austin in the
final chapters of *The Early History of Institutions*.
Holmes thought Darwin the seminal influence of the

---

[12] Woodward, *The Doctor's Disciples*, 54. The German *savants*
were not universally popular. Leslie Stephen wrote in 1876 :
" Nations differ widely in their mode of expressing self-
satisfaction, but hardly in the degree of complacency. A
German, perhaps, is the most priggish in his consciousness of
merit. He expounds his theory of world-history with the airs
of a professor and lays down his superiority to all mankind as
the latest discovery of scientific thought " (*Men, Books and
Mountains*, 148).

[13] See Lectures II and V, *infra*.

[14] In 14 L.Q.R. 219, Pollock, in an obituary, saluted Challis as
" one of the last conveyancers of the old school,"

century. " No one," he wrote, " has done so much to affect our whole way of thinking about the universe." [15] Maitland saluted Savigny not only as the Romanist and as the historian, but as " the herald of evolution, the man who substitutes development for manufacture, organism for mechanism, natural laws for Natural Law, the man who is nervously afraid lest a code should impede the beautiful processes of natural growth." [16]

The ever-increasing interest in historical and especially in medieval studies that spread over Victorian scholarship might have been expected to make a peculiar appeal to the English lawyer with his proud consciousness of continuity and his unique records. Yet the response was desultory and belated. Among the practitioners this was, perhaps, not altogether surprising, though there were distinguished exceptions. Serjeant Manning was a medievalist and pressed his learning into service both as reporter and as counsel.[17] Mr. Justice Willes, here as elsewhere, was pre-eminent. It was he who sent Pollock to the Year Books and set him " on the path of discovery that modern English law cannot be properly understood without going back to its medieval origins and development." [18] But even in academic circles Maine was at first a lonely missionary. It was not until the last quarter of the nineteenth century that legal history became the subject

---

[15] *Pollock-Holmes Letters*, I, 58.

[16] *Introduction to Gierke, Political Theories of the Middle Age*, XV

[17] Manning (1781–1866) made his reports a repository of learning. For an example of his arguments at the bar, see *Bruce* v. *Wait* (1840) 1 M.&G. 1.

[18] Pollock, *For my Grandson*, 166. See also *Pollock–Holmes Letters*, II, 112.

of serious study. Sir Kenelm Digby was a pioneer when in 1875 he based the first elementary exposition of Real Property upon original sources and applied to the land law the methods so triumphantly exploited by Stubbs in constitutional history.[19] His example was eagerly followed. In 1885 Pike introduced new methods of editing the Year Books [20]; in 1887 the Selden Society was founded; and in 1895 medieval scholarship flowered in Pollock and Maitland's *History of English Law before the time of Edward I.*

As Maine's career shows, historical and comparative jurisprudence are near akin. The common lawyers, if they found it less fatiguing to be proud of their past than to know it, had long paid something more than lip service to the advantages of comparative law. Before the reign of Victoria they had frequently sought French analogies, and especially in Pothier and the Code Civile. But here as in other fields France was forced to yield to Germany. Already in the early years of the nineteenth century Austin had leant heavily upon Savigny; and it is curious that, after Austin abandoned his course, German influence took so long to creep into the interstices of English law. The Americans were quicker to change their allegiance. At Harvard historical jurisprudence was taught by a

---

[19] Digby was a man of parts. Born in 1836, he was appointed in 1868 to the new Vinerian Readership in Civil and Common Law. From 1874 to 1892 he practised mainly before the Privy Council. In 1892 he became a county court judge. In 1895 he resigned and became Permanent Under-Secretary to the Home Office.

[20] The Rolls Series of the Year Books began in 1863, but it was Pike who first saw and grasped his opportunities.

pupil of Savigny from 1848 to 1850 [21]; and in the latter year the young American prodigy, William Wetmore Story, wrote to Lowell of his remarkable experiences in Berlin.[22] " Von Savigny, the celebrated jurist, I have seen repeatedly, and I can assure you that of all petrifactions he is the most remarkable. He is as dry as dust. Very courteous and affable and complimentary I found him, but living wholly in a book-world and that book-world a law-book-world. He held up both his hands when he found out that I was an artist, and cried out, ' What, an artist and a lawyer ! That is impossible.' " In England the infiltration was slow. As late as 1875 Markby complained that eyes were still fixed upon the decadent French and earnestly recommended students to turn to Germany. Markby practised what he preached [23]; but he was now preaching to the converted. The young jurists were eager to imbibe the new culture. Pollock was introduced by Bryce to Savigny as to " the greatest expounder of legal principles in modern Europe." [24] Maitland discovered him without assistance and said that it was he who first showed him " the

---

[21] Pound, *The Formative Era of American Law*, 50. The pupil was L. S. Cushing, who had himself translated *Savigny on Possession.*

[22] Henry James, *William Wetmore Story and his Friends*, 215–216. W. W. Story (1819–95) was the son of Mr. Justice Story and was himself a remarkable man. Before he was 28 he had written a *Law of Contracts* in two volumes of 1,000 pages each and a *Treatise on Sales of Personal Property*. He then abandoned the United States and the law for Italy and sculpture.

[23] See his *Elements of Law*, first published in 1871, and the supplement of 1875.

[24] Pollock, *For my Grandson*, 169. In the Preface to his *First Book of Jurisprudence* (1896) he declared that " among the authors of past generations I owe most to Savigny."

way in which law should be regarded." [25] At the close of the century, it is true, voices were heard of deprecation if not of dissent. Pollock and Maitland both came to temper their admiration with criticism. But Savigny was still the master whom to the end both delighted to honour.

Such was the background to the judicial and juristic work of Victoria's reign. But notwithstanding the attraction of scientific and evolutionary studies, despite the " march of mind " and the " climate of opinion " and the many facile phrases that serve as substitutes for thought, it remains a vulgar error to suppose that any " influence " can itself produce books, decide cases and command events. Law, no more than any other human creation, is the automatic result of natural forces or intellectual movements. It is made by men. Whatever the pitfalls, it is less misleading to adopt or adapt Carlyle's creed and approach legal history through biography. English lawyers, of all men, should believe in the power of the great judge. Would the common law have been the same had Bacon and not Coke stood at the parting of the sixteenth and the seventeenth centuries, had William Murray not been " caught young " or had Lord Campbell overlooked Colin Blackburn ?

The judicial history of the reign may be surveyed in three periods. From 1837 to 1852 the Bench was dominated by Baron Parke. The son of a Liverpool merchant, he distinguished himself at Trinity College,

[25] Fisher, *F. W. Maitland*, 18. Maitland began, but did not complete, a translation of Savigny's *Geschichte des Römischen Rechts*.

Cambridge, of which he became a Fellow. He was then for seven years a special pleader and, when at last called to the Bar, had an immediate and striking success. From 1828 to 1834 he was a judge of the King's Bench and from 1834 to 1855 a Baron of the Exchequer, where he made the court his own. In 1856 he was translated, as Lord Wensleydale, to the House of Lords and died, still in office, in 1868. His judgments reveal the diverse and sometimes inconsistent strands interwoven in the professional mind. Lord Mansfield was praised by Dr. Johnson for not being "a mere lawyer": he made law serve life. To Baron Parke law was sometimes the servant and sometimes the master. His early experience tempted him to cherish too tenderly the pleader's craft and to approach a case as if it were an exercise in mathematics for failure in which the hapless litigant must pay. But when he averted his eyes from process he was masterly, quick to penetrate the core of a problem, unerring in the extraction of principle from precedent and endowed with the gift of lucid exposition. The two sides of his personality not unnaturally impressed contemporaries with distaste or delight according to their several tastes. Chief Baron Pollock, for twenty years his colleague, denied him the attributes of greatness. He was only, he insisted, "a considerable man. His intellectual powers were like the explosive compositions called 'fulminating'—very powerful within a limited sphere." [26] Lord Coleridge, recalling him in later life, allowed his superb qualities but lamented their dissipation upon the "absurdities of special pleading." He had heard

[26] Lord Hanworth, *Lord Chief Baron Pollock*, 196–197.

him " rejoice at non-suiting a plaintiff in an undefended cause, saying, with a sort of triumphant air, that those who drew loose declarations brought scandal on the law." [27] But the testimony on the other side is weighty. Mr. Justice Willes placed the law " under greater obligations to him than to any judge within living memory." [28] Baron Martin, the son-in-law of Chief Baron Pollock and testifying therefore against interest, acclaimed him " without doubt the ablest and best public servant I was personally acquainted with in the whole course of my life." [29] Now that the dust has settled on the pages of special pleading and Baron Parke is read for his contributions to the substantive law, the verdict of posterity is emphatically in his favour. He was to Lord Dunedin the " absolute ideal of a judge." [30]

The years between the Common Law Procedure Act of 1852 and the Judicature Act of 1875 saw a succession of great judges. Of the many candidates for the First Class the most remarkable figure narrowly to miss the highest honours was Lord Campbell. The son of a Scots minister and destined himself for the ministry, he forsook the manse for London and the law. To pay his way, while he devoted his days to learning, he gave his nights to journalism. As a reporter

---

[27] *The Law in* 1847 *and the Law in* 1889, a paper read by Lord Coleridge in 1889 to the " Law Students at Birmingham " and reprinted in *The Contemporary Review*, Vol. 57, p. 797.

[28] Handsomely cited by Lord Coleridge in his paper: *ibid.*, pp. 799–801.

[29] *Lord Derby* v. *Bury Improvement Commissioners* (1868) L.R.3 Ex. 133.

[30] See *Fifty Years*, pp. 142–148.

he was ubiquitous, passing undeterred from Westminster Hall to the more doubtful purlieus of Covent
Garden and Drury Lane. He wrote indiscriminately
as occasion offered or interest suggested [31]; and his
magnum opus, the Lives of the Lord Chancellors and
of the Chief Justices, though deft and lively, are mem-
orials not of pride but of prejudice.[32] When at length
he, too, became successively Chief Justice and Lord
Chancellor, he proved, somewhat against expectation,
to be an able and resolute judge. Had he reached
office earlier in life and had he learned to discipline his
tongue, he might have achieved greatness.

To three judges of the golden age, Bramwell,
Blackburn and Willes, greatness cannot be denied.[33]
Lord Bramwell was the most single-minded of men.
Neither by nature nor nurture a scholar, he began his
working life as a clerk in his father's bank; and, with
an instinctive grasp of commercial realities, he yet
sought to trace in the business man's contract the
reflection, however distorted, of the political economy
to whose classical canons he was ever faithful. Not
learned in the environs of jurisprudence, he accumulated
a prodigious knowledge of the cases but refused to be
bullied by precedent into any conclusion that seemed
to him contrary to principle or justice. On the Bench
he was the embodiment of common sense in law. He

[31] He tried, *inter alia*, to prove that Shakespeare was once an
attorney: see his *Shakespeare's Legal Acquirements*.
[32] See the strictures of Pollock C.B. in Lord Hanworth's *Lord
Chief Baron Pollock*, 202–205.
[33] Bramwell and Blackburn both continued in office after 1875,
but it was in the years between 1852 and 1875 that their repu-
tations were made.

wasted no words, [34] suffered no irrelevance and stated his conclusions without refinement and without compromise.

Blackburn was in many ways the antithesis of Bramwell. From Eton and Trinity he went to the Bar, where for twenty years he was but moderately successful. In 1845 he published his *Treatise on the Contract of Sale*. A learned and original book and an early essay in comparative law, it revealed a cast of mind not always practical and one that must have suggested qualms to those attorneys who preferred to brief counsel whom they could more readily understand. In 1859 his appointment to the Queen's Bench took the profession by surprise. The story is well known, but may be re-told in the words of Lord Campbell who chose him and who had to repel the charge of having turned a duty into a job. " July 3, 1859. I have already got into great disgrace by disposing of my judicial patronage on the principle *detur digniori*. Having occasion for a new judge, I appointed Blackburn, the fittest man in Westminster Hall, although wearing a stuff gown ; whereas several Whig Q.C.s and M.P.s were considering which of them would be the man, not dreaming that they could all be passed over. They got me well abused in *The Times* and other newspapers, but Lyndhurst has defended me gallantly in the House of Lords." [35] Blackburn at once justified his choice

---

[34] On one occasion a ruffian had been convicted before him of an atrocious assault. He began to address him as was usual before passing sentence in a serious case. The prisoner interrupted. " How much ? " he asked. " Eight years," said Bramwell, " Next case."

[35] *Life of Lord Campbell*, II, 372–373. Lord Lyndhurst, in his speech, referred to the heading of *The Times* leader, " Who is

and was a great power on the Bench for a quarter of a century.[36] He had a brusque manner that concealed some inner doubts. He was not always ruthless to break through authority so as to reach and assert principle and to do justice. There was perhaps enough of the academic in him to pore too anxiously upon all sides of the question: some at least of his judgments are thus flawed.[37] But, when all deductions are made, he remains one of the great common lawyers of all time.

Bramwell was the son of an English banker and Blackburn a Scot. Willes was Irish. Unlike Blackburn, he won an immediate success at the Bar and, though he, too, never took silk, his gifts were universally acknowledged. He was counsel both for the Treasury and for Lloyd's, and his seniors were accustomed to take notes of his arguments in court.[38] From 1855, when he was made a judge of the Common Pleas, to 1872, when he had a nervous collapse and shot himself, he was supreme. He shared Blackburn's mastery of the reports and his knowledge of foreign jurisprudence, and he added a living interest in the Year Books.[39] While Blackburn was rough in personal relations and too often hesitant on the Bench, Willes—in private life shy, reserved and *gauche*—was firm and confident in

Mr. Blackburn ? ", and prophesied that the answer would soon be clear. He was supported by Lord Wensleydale.

[36] According to Pollock, when Blackburn finally retired in 1886, he said " Damn the law " and read nothing but French novels: *Pollock–Holmes Letters*, II, 306.

[37] *e.g. River Wear Commissioners* v. *Adamson* (1877) 2 App.Cas. 743, and *Foakes* v. *Beer* (1884) 9 App.Cas. at pp. 614–623.

[38] See Ashton, *As I went on my Way*, 23–26.

[39] *Supra*, p. 9. He was an accomplished scholar outside the law and a linguist with an exceptional knowledge of Spanish: Pollock, *For my Godson*, 164–167.

judicial decision. In retrospect his judgments are seen to be masterpieces. All aspects of a case have been reviewed, all arguments weighed and all authorities examined. But the mind has sifted and selected, and the result is the exposition and settlement of a principle so simple and convincing that, once revealed by the master, it seems strange that it had not hitherto been perceived. It is not without cause that Sir Frederick Pollock dedicated his *Law of Torts* to him as to a judge " wise and valiant."

The years from 1875 to 1901, if not, like the two preceding decades, conspicuously an age of creation, added at least three names to the roll of great judges.[40] Lindley, who was born in 1828 and survived to 1921, was conspicuously the child of his time. He was the son of a Professor of Botany at University College, London, where he himself was educated. He studied Roman law at Bonn and translated Thibaut's *System des Pandektenrechts* under the title *Introduction to the Study of Jurisprudence*. In 1860 he published his celebrated *Treatise on the Law of Partnership, including its application to Companies*. In 1875 Lord Cairns, as if to symbolise the catholic jurisdiction of the new High Court of Justice, made him, though a Chancery practitioner, a judge of the Common Pleas Division. Here, and later in the Court of Appeal and in the House of Lords, he was the most versatile of lawyers,

---

[40] Lord Cairns enjoyed very great contemporary reputation, but it is doubtful if it stands as high today. Unrivalled in the marshalling of facts, his judgments give the impression of aridity. Where he competed with Blackburn, as in *Rylands* v. *Fletcher* (1868) L.R. 3 H.L. 330 and in *Cundy* v. *Lindsay* (1878) 3 App.Cas.459, he does not appear to advantage.

equally at home at common law and in equity, and, like Blackburn before him, he could claim to be both judge and jurist. Pollock, his grateful pupil, dedicated his *Contract* to him as he had dedicated his *Torts* to Willes.

Charles Bowen was, *par excellence*, the prize scholar. He won the Arnold Historical Prize, the Hertford and the Ireland Scholarships, and became in 1857 a Fellow of Balliol. Thirty years later, now a Lord Justice of Appeal, he translated into English verse the *Eclogues* and the first six books of the *Aeneid*. He preferred, indeed, to air his scholarship outside the law and dismissed with disdain the suggestion that he should write a textbook.[41] But a judge's memorial must be sought in his judgments, and these bear on every page the mark of the scholar. His mind was subtle, sceptical and caustic. He once said that " he had read Maine's works with the profoundest admiration for the genius of the author but with just a faint suspicion somewhere in the background of his mind that the results might turn out to be all nonsense." [42] Nor, if need be, did he spare his colleagues. The judges were once discussing the draft of an address to the Queen. To the words " Conscious as we are of our shortcomings " it was objected that they ill fitted the dignity of the Bench. " Suppose," said Bowen, " that we substitute ' Conscious as we are of one another's shortcomings.' " [43] The man thus revealed was too remote from the bustle of life to be at ease with juries.

[41] Cunningham, *Lord Bowen*, 164.
[42] Leslie Stephen, *Life of Sir Fitz James Stephen*, 413.
[43] Cunningham, *Lord Bowen*, 183.

He could not put himself in their place and he over-rated their intelligence.[44]   But his judgments display a mastery of the law expressed in fastidious prose; and a Court of Appeal of which he, Lindley and Lord Justice Fry were the members challenges comparison with any before or since.[45]

Lord Macnaghten was an Ulsterman, educated first at Trinity College, Dublin, and then at Trinity College, Cambridge. He was both scholar and athlete. He was the senior Classic of his year and twice rowed in the Boat Race. He won the Chancellor's medal and the Diamond Sculls. For many years he was a busy member of the Chancery Bar and a Conservative member of Parliament; and in 1887 he succeeded Blackburn as a Lord of Appeal, a promotion then unprecedented. Like Lindley, he was as happy with the common law as with equity. Unlike Blackburn, " he had the gifts of listening with patience and deciding without doubt." [46] Two qualities are conspicuous in his judgments: the power to strip from a doctrine the incrustations of time, leaving it for future use naked and unashamed, and an exquisite sense of literary form. He could edge with irony the keenest observation

---

[44] He once prosecuted a burglar who had been caught on the roof of the prosecutor's house with the tools of his trade in his hands. " If, gentlemen of the jury," he said, " you think that the accused was on the roof of the house to enjoy the midnight breeze and, by pure accident, happened to have about him the necessary tools of a housebreaker, with no dishonest intention of employing them, you will, of course, acquit him." The jury promptly took him at his word. Cunningham, *Lord Bowen*, 115.

[45] It may be paralleled in the present century by the combination of Lord Justices Bankes, Scrutton and Atkin.

[46] See Lord Sumner's life of Macnaghten in the D.N.B.

and adorn with elegance the most robust of minds.[47]

One characteristic was shared by all the judges from Parke to Macnaghten: none had a legal education. There was none to have. Until 1852, when the Common Law Procedure Act furnished at once the need and the opportunity for judges to think in terms of principle, there was no serious study of the law at the Universities, and the old professional training in the Inns of Court had long disappeared. " Dining in Hall was the only survival, and it was almost literally true that a man ate his way to the Bar." [48] Save for Blackstone, whether in the authorised version or as revised by Serjeant Stephen in 1841, there were few books which an intelligent man with a mind above drudgery could attempt to read without dismay or disgust. [49] A witness before the Oxford University Commission of 1852 described the " usual routine of what is now called a legal education." [50] A young man, " entered at one of the Inns of Court, is received as a pupil for a year by some eminent conveyancer to whom he gives a hundred guineas for the privilege of going daily to his chambers . . . He finds that he has purchased the right of

[47] *e.g.*, his judgments in *Van Grutten* v. *Foxwell* [1897] A.C. 658 and *Reddaway* v. *Bonham* [1896] A.C. 199.

[48] Council of Legal Education, *Calendar*, p. 2. In University College, London, despite the brave efforts of Austin, the attempt to teach law had achieved slight success. See Prof. G. W. Keeton, 51 *Juridical Review*, 120.

[49] Three exceptions may be noted: Joshua Williams' *Real Property* (1845), Blackburn's *Contract of Sale* (1845) and Stephen on *Pleading* (1824), where, if the subject repelled, the treatment might please a devotee.

[50] Report of the Oxford University Commission (1852), 197–200. The witness was S. C. Denison, once Stowell Fellow of University College, Oxford, and Deputy Judge Advocate General.

walking blindfold into a sort of legal jungle. Masses
of papers are placed daily before him, every sheet of
which contains numberless terms as new and strange
to him as the words of a foreign language and the
bare meaning of which he rarely arrives at before the
clerk announces that the client has called to take the
papers away. . . . This unpropitious year at length
over, the youth is doomed to go through a second year
of the like probation, at the same cost and almost as
unprofitably, in the chambers of a special pleader or an
equity draftsman; and by the end of that year he is
so bedevilled and so wearied that he gives up the attempt
as hopeless and becomes a clergyman (an event of
extremely common occurrence with Oxford men)."
Such disillusion, if not a similar fate, awaited most
men who later became eminent as judge or jurist.
Sir FitzJames Stephen " was for a time in the chambers
of Mr. Field (afterwards Lord Field), then the leading
junior on the Midland Circuit; but it was on the
distinct understanding that he was to receive no instruction from his tutor." He then went into the
chambers of a conveyancer. "I worked very hard
with him, but I was incapable of being taught and he
of teaching." [51] Lord Bowen, looking back upon
his initiation into the law, remembered only " the white-
washed misery of the pupil's room and the hopeless
dinginess of the occupations of its inhabitants." " So
bitter is the thought of it," he said, " that death itself
can hardly be more bitter." [52] Sir Frederick Pollock
was redeemed from bondage only by his good fortune

[51] Leslie Stephen, *Life of Sir FitzJames Stephen*, 118–119.
[52] Cunningham, *Lord Bowen*, 76–77.

in becoming a pupil of Lindley and a marshal to Willes.[53]

It is true that the publication of *Smith's Leading Cases* [54] offered the determined adventurer a *tabula in naufragio* and that considerable if desultory learning could be gleaned from the reports prepared by such men as Alderson, Blackburn, Campbell and Maule. But, like Scott's hero in the first chapter of *Waverley*, though less agreeably, the pupil could be conscious only of " driving through a sea of books, like a vessel without pilot or rudder." Nor must it be supposed that the absence of organised education was felt by the profession as a reproach. The problems of litigation were to be solved, not in sedate seclusion by those who scanned the battle from afar, but more strenuously by those who lived in the thick of it and who knew by close and grim experience what legal conflict really meant. As late as 1883 Dicey sensed the predominant professional opinion to be little altered. " If the question whether English law can be taught at the Universities could be submitted in the form of a case to a body of eminent counsel, there is no doubt whatever as to what would be their answer. They would reply with unanimity and without hesitation that English law must be learned and cannot be taught and that the only places where it can be learned are the law courts or chambers." [55] Dicey, it must be added,

---

[53] Pollock, *For my Godson*, 161–162.
[54] First published in 1837, with the avowed object of helping the student. The third and fourth editions, in 1847 and 1850, were prepared by Willes and Keating.
[55] Dicey, Inaugural Lecture, " Can English Law be taught at the Universities?", delivered at Oxford, April 21, 1883. He

was speaking of those then prominent at the Bar or already on the Bench; and he was careful to mark the new era inaugurated for their successors in the second half of the century.

The renaissance began simultaneously in the Inns of Court and at the Universities. In the Inns of Court a scheme of education was adopted in 1852 largely through the pressure exercised by the formidable if acid personality of Lord Westbury. Five Readers were appointed, of whom the most prominent was Sir Henry Maine. In 1853 the first and voluntary examination was held and seven candidates attended. In 1872 the examination was made essential for call to the Bar. Many men, later distinguished judges, served as lecturers and examiners; among them were Sir FitzJames Stephen, Lord Davey and Lord Sumner. But, after Lord Westbury had given the original impetus and had served indefatigably as Chairman for twenty-one years, Lord Macnaghten's association with the Council of Legal Education was perhaps the closest and the most inspiring. He was an examiner in 1864 and Chairman from 1895 to 1913.[56]

The history of nineteenth-century Oxford illustrates the awakening of the Universities.[57] A hesitant step was taken in 1850 by the creation of a new and combined

---

noted, at pp. 28–29, that in the United States they ordered these things better.

[56] See Council of Legal Education, *Calendar*, 1–5. I am indebted for much information and for access to the records to the kindness of my friend, T. Harvatt, Esq., Barrister-at-law, Secretary and Assistant Director to the Council of Legal Education.

[57] The similar experiences at Cambridge are described by Winstanley, *Later Victorian Cambridge*, 206–208.

school of Jurisprudence and Modern History. In the next year Convocation established a serious examination for the degree of Bachelor of Civil Law. The " disputations " which it replaced are described by G. V. Cox, Esquire Bedel, who had himself taken part in them. [58] A question was proposed to each candidate: *Quid existimas de hac quaestione, An dominium acquiri possit sine possessione* ? The necessary and traditional arguments, in appropriate Latin, were then handed to the " disputants " and, to occupy the hour prescribed by the statutes, they were accommodated with a folio *Justinian* and the relevant references. At the end of the hour the presiding examiner, who had meanwhile passed the time according to his taste, dismissed the candidates with the single word *Sufficit*. In 1852 the report of the University Commission was received. All concerned, members and witnesses alike, deplored the existing lethargy, but they differed upon the remedy. Baron Parke urged the University to teach " the elements of legal science before the young men engaged in the complex and difficult details of its practice." Lord Westbury preferred all legal education, preliminary and advanced, to be the monopoly of the Inns of Court. The Commissioners decided to support Baron Parke so that undergraduates might be spared the " temptations and distractions of London life."[59] Solicitude for the tender plants raised at Oxford was doubtless proper, but behind it a nice and more intractable problem was posed. Could law be used both as an instrument

[58] Cox, *Recollections of Oxford*, Feb. 25, 1851.
[59] Report of University Commission (1852), 75–78.

of general education and as a technical training? It was, indeed, not necessary to assume, with Savigny, that law was incompatible with culture; [60] but the University must decide whether it was to be offered as one of several roads to intellectual discipline or whether it was to be a first step on the professional ladder.

At length in 1871 a separate School of Jurisprudence was established. In the same year James Bryce delivered his Inaugural Lecture as Regius Professor of Civil Law. When, as in duty bound, he recommended the study of Roman Law, he did not preach to deaf ears, though he may be thought to have opened his case in extravagant terms. He felt it incumbent upon him, or at least desirable, to rebuke contemporary judges for their lack of " literary culture and polished taste " and to warn them that, if they wished not merely to be learned but even to remain honest, they should embrace the science, philosophy and ethics of the Roman jurists. [61] In the syllabus of the new School, therefore, it was neither surprising nor unhappy that its academic character should be emphasised. It included papers on the Institutes of Gaius and Justinian, on International Law and on General Jurisprudence as understood by Bentham and Austin. The study of English law was confined to Constitutional History,

---

[60] *Supra*, p. 11.

[61] Bryce, *The Academical Study of the Civil Law*, Feb. 25, 1871. At p. 36 he says: " It is scarcely possible that a corrupt administration of justice can co-exist with an abstract enthusiasm for the propriety and elegance of law as a science such as existed among the great jurists of Rome." If the reflection upon the English Bench was unfortunate, the sentiment itself, while noble, may be thought somewhat too credulous a generalisation from Continental models.

exemplified by Stubbs' Charters, and to the History of Real Property. Contemporary Law was ignored.[62] It may be said with some confidence that the School served its time well by bridging the gulf, hitherto dark and deep, between a liberal education and the mysteries of a craft.

The new academic interest in law provoked, and was itself sustained by, a new style of textbook, devoted primarily to the exposition of principle and designed especially for students. The first-fruits of this learning were gathered in the field of contract. Leake in 1867 made an heroic attempt to approach the subject scientifically and to see it as a coherent whole. In the preface to his *Law of Contracts* he observed that there existed no " English work undertaken with the exclusive object of treating Contract in its general and abstract form, apart from its specific practical applications " ; and this gap he endeavoured to fill.[63] But it was in the next decade that two books revolutionised the teaching of English law. In 1876 Sir Frederick Pollock [64] published his *Principles of Contract*. He sought, in harmony with the Judicature Acts, to examine the

---

[62] *Oxford University Gazette*, Dec. 12, 1871. The B.C.L. syllabus (*O.U. Gazette*, July 6, 1872) catered to some extent for English lawyers. Beside Roman Law, Jurisprudence and International Law, two special subjects were to be chosen from the English Law of Property, Contract, Torts, Equity, Criminal Law and Evidence.

[63] Stephen Martin Leake, who had been forced by deafness to retire from practice in 1863, was, with Bullen, the author of the celebrated *Precedents on Pleading*, first published in 1860.

[64] He was born in the purple of the law. His grandfather, who had twenty-four children, was Lord Chief Baron Pollock; his father was Queen's Remembrancer; his cousin, as Lord Hanworth, became Master of the Rolls. He himself was content to be Judge of the Admiralty Court of the Cinque Ports.

inter-play of law and equity, and he set the results
not only against Roman, Continental and American
models, but also against the Indian Contract Act,
from which it might be supposed, insular eccentricities
had been eliminated.[65] In his interpretation of the
Roman Law he acknowledged and accepted the
influence and opinions of Savigny. In 1879 Sir William
Anson [66] published his *Law of Contract*. He was,
even more fervently than Pollock, the disciple of
Savigny, and it was through the superior vision of the
master that he hoped to irradiate the concepts of
obligation and agreement and to correct the English
astigmatism. With these two books the foundations
of the new learning were laid; and the inauguration
in 1884 of the Law Quarterly Review emphasised its
importance in professional as in academic circles.

Too much, however, must not be expected too
soon. Queen Victoria's judges had been brought up
in an older school and, while they might sympathise
with youthful enthusiasm, could scarcely be diverted

---

[65] The Indian Contract Act had a chequered history. It was
drafted in 1864 by a number of Commissioners, including
W. M. James, afterwards Lord James of Hereford. In 1867
it was introduced by Maine as Law member of the Governor-
General's Council, though he disliked some of its provisions.
When in 1869 Sir FitzJames Stephen succeeded Maine, he
re-drafted the first fifty clauses which he thought " very crude,"
and it was passed in 1872. Pollock later criticised it with some
severity: see Pollock and Mulla, *Indian Contract Act*, and
infra, p. 122.

[66] Though it is recorded that he once earned two guineas at
quarter sessions, Anson was essentially an academic lawyer.
In addition to his *Contract* and his *Law and Custom of the
Constitution*, he wrote *Ballades en terms de la ley*, verses designed
to " instruct undergraduates hoping to get a First Class in
the School of Jurisprudence or a high place in the examination
for the B.C.L. degree ": *Memoir of Sir William Anson*, 84–90.

by it. Only in the next century were the men destined for the Bench to be bred upon Anson and Pollock. One of the first and greatest of the new generation was Lord Justice Scrutton. His was a career at which Parke or Bowen would have stared and might, or might not, have envied. After obtaining a First Class in the Law Tripos at Cambridge, he became a Bachelor of Laws in the University of London and Barstow Scholar in the Inns of Court. While reading in chambers he was Professor of Constitutional Law and Legal History at University College, London. Four times he won the Yorke Prize for a Legal Essay and upon such diverse topics as Copyright, Commons and Common Fields and the Influence of Roman Law on the Laws of England. He crowned his literary achievements by the completion in 1886 of his book on *Charter Parties*, to become at once the standard work.

It was natural, and perhaps inevitable, that the English writers should have drawn their inspiration from Continental jurists. But the results were not wholly happy. The *a priori* postulates of German scholars were not easy to apply to the tough and empirical fragments of case law, and they sometimes deflected, and even distorted, the instinctive grasp of practical needs and limitations which, whatever the defects of its qualities, made English law eminently serviceable. This incompatibility marred the work of Anson. Impelled by his admiration of Savigny to explain English, no less than German, doctrine in language fit for the ears of philosophers, he emphasised consent, and even more pedantically *Consensus*, as the one root of contract. As an initial assumption it might pass muster: as the major premise of a syllogism it was perilous. One cause, at least, of the perplexities that have long darkened the treatment of mistake was Anson's insistence that it must be an exercise upon the theme of Real Consent. Pollock, though he at first shared the illusion, soon remembered that he was, after all, an English lawyer; and in the third edition of his book, published in 1881, he preferred to offer as the basis of contract the " reasonable expectation of the parties." [67] If such a phenomenon as a national character does in truth exist and if in any degree it colours or shapes the jurisprudence of a country, it is surely this presumption rather than the alien *consensus* that suits the temper of the common law.

---

[67] Many years later, on August 10, 1920, Pollock wrote to Holmes: " It is rather amusing to see your new lights trumpeting reasonable expectation as the real fundamental conception in contract. I agree, of course, having put it in my 3rd edition nearly forty years ago, only without a trumpet obligato ": *Pollock–Holmes Letters*, II, 48.

Chapter 2

CIVIL LIABILITY

IT is fair to say that, when Victoria came to the throne, the necessity, or indeed the propriety, of determining the principles of civil liability had not occurred either to judge or to jurist. Blackstone, in the third volume of his *Commentaries*, had distinguished personal actions into those founded on contracts and those founded on torts, and he had surveyed, without scientific pretension but with characteristic lucidity, some of the ground familiar to modern readers. In 1836 Serjeant Stephen had announced his design " of composing a work on the Laws of England to which the text of Blackstone should be in a great measure contributory "; and he had resolved, not without intelligible misgiving, to " discard all solicitude about the measure of my adherence to the original work and to interweave my own composition with it as freely as the purpose of general improvement might seem to require." But audacity, or perhaps discernment, failed him. In torts, at least, he cannot be said to have " improved " upon Blackstone. Co-ordination was still wanting: the disciple succeeded only in clouding the master's clarity and distinction.[1]

---

[1] As late as 1874, when the seventh edition of Stephen's *Commentaries* was published, little had been altered or amended. The reader in search of " torts " had to peruse two chapters sandwiched between a survey of the courts and a treatise upon pleading.

The core of the problem was the treatment of negligence. Blackstone had been content with a casual and curious digression in the midst of "implied contracts."[2] But when in 1780 he died, the question had become urgent. The new roads were crossing England; and, in accord with the apparent axiom that disaster is the price of human invention, the unwonted ease of communication multiplied accidents and fertilised litigation. To harvest the rich crop of running-down actions, the judges were forced to recognise negligence as a distinct species of Case. They were nevertheless determined not to allow a remedy simply because the defendant had been careless. So wide and vague a liability had somehow to be disciplined. They therefore insisted that damage carelessly caused might be redressed only if, in the circumstances of any given case, the defendant could be said to owe the plaintiff a duty to be careful.[3] The device at once narrowed the legal range of negligence; but it remained to enumerate, if not to rationalise, the situations in which the law would impose the duty of care. This task was more formidable. It could be completed only by a protracted course of trial and error, and it engaged the energies of the judges for another hundred years.

The courts were initially distracted by Blackstone's antithesis between actions founded on contracts and those on torts. Were these actions mutually exclusive? If, in the course of fulfilling a contract between two persons, a third were injured, could his claim be

[2] *Commentaries*, III, 163–165.
[3] See *Govett* v. *Radnidge* (1802) 3 East 62.

repelled as beyond the ambit of the contract? These questions became insistent amid the new perils of a mechanical age. The railways seemed, at least in popular imagination, even more potent instruments of destruction than the curricles that bowled so merrily along the turnpike roads, and they tempted plaintiffs with the prospect of still wealthier defendants. The judicial reaction may be seen in such a case as *Austin* v. *Great Western Railway Co.*[4] The defendants were bound by statute to carry children under three years of age without charge and were entitled to half the adult fare for children between three and five. The plaintiff was aged three years and two months. His mother, carrying him in her arms, took a ticket for herself but none for him, and, in the ensuing action, her omission was deemed maternal rather than fraudulent. Through the defendants' negligence there was a collision and the plaintiff was injured. The court agreed that he might recover damages; but, while the majority assumed, somewhat disingenuously, that the contract between the defendants and the mother " operated in the child's favour," Mr. Justice Blackburn disdained sophistry. The right of a passenger to safe carriage rested, not upon contract, but upon a duty of care imposed by the law.

The railways were doubtless inviting targets, and there were precedents for the liability of common carriers that could be pressed into service and applied to the carriage of passengers. Elsewhere the dilemma was more painful. To allow a third party to sue a

[4] (1867) L.R. 2 Q.B. 442. See also *Marshall* v. *York, Newcastle and Berwick Ry. Co.* (1851) 11 C.B. 655.

defendant who had acted solely in pursuance of a contract was inelegant. At least where the contract was of a more intimate character than that of a railway company, the judges were reluctant to extend its rights to a stranger. They were especially anxious to confine the incidence of contracts of sale and of work and maintenance. Their attitude is sufficiently indicated by the case of *Winterbottom* v. *Wright*.[5] The defendant had contracted with the Postmaster-General to supply a coach and to keep it in good repair. Owing to his negligence the coach broke down while the plaintiff, a coachman, was driving it, and the plaintiff was injured. Counsel on each side drew vivid analogies from the contemporary scene. For the plaintiff the court was invited to envisage a contract to repair a church or a workhouse and the task was so badly performed that stones fell upon the heads of paterfamilias or pauper. Were such characteristic victims to be denied redress ? Byles for the defendant stressed the lessons of a recent French disaster. If the present plaintiff were to succeed, " every one of the sufferers by such an accident as that which happened on the Versailles railway might have his action against the manufacturer of the defective axle." The sturdy conservatism of Byles prevailed. The court recoiled from the vision of wholesale litigation and gave judgment for the defendant.

A special group of cases, unembarrassed by the intrusion of contract, lights the narrow path of duty which the judges had to tread. How far and in what

[5] (1842) 10 M. & W. 109. In the twentieth century it has become fashionable to explain the decision on the technical ground that the plaintiff had declared in contract. But the report shows that the court was substantially influenced by policy.

circumstances was an occupier liable to persons who entered his premises and were injured owing to their defective condition ? The solution of this, as of any other problem in the common law, demanded a supply of victims for judicial experiment. Inhibited from academic speculation, the judge must await the initiative of the litigant. Medical science can rely on a succession of blood donors: legal research still awaits devotees ardent enough to risk their limbs if not their lives upon doubtful issues. It must be accounted a happy chance that between 1856 and 1867 a gratifying number of plaintiffs succumbed to an agreeable variety of accidents.

Alternative tests were suggested by judges trying to pick their way through tangled facts to legal conclusions. On the one hand they might examine the status of the plaintiff and the reason for his presence on the defendant's premises. Not all entrants should be treated alike: a burglar must, in more senses than one, take things as he found them. But even between lawful visitors it was possible to discriminate. An occupier might reasonably be expected to show more solicitude for a person with whom he wished to do business than for one whose presence he was content to tolerate. On the other hand stress might be laid, not on the occasion of the entrance, but on the conduct of the defendant, and a distinction drawn between active negligence and the passive state of the premises, between misfeasance and nonfeasance.

In *Southcote* v. *Stanley*,[6] the first case of the series, both tests were canvassed. The declaration stated that the defendant had an hotel, that " he had permitted

[6] (1856) 1 H. & N. 247.

and invited the plaintiff to enter it as a visitor," that a glass door was unsafe and that, while the plaintiff was seeking to open it, the glass fell out and injured him. The action failed, but for a variety of reasons. Chief Baron Pollock observed that the plaintiff was not a paying guest but a gratuitous visitor and, " like a member of the defendant's household, must take his chance." Baron Alderson refused the analogy, pressed upon him in argument, of a shop and its customers: persons who came on business deserved more care than " those who came by invitation." To Baron Bramwell all lawful visitors looked alike, and it was necessary to ask of what they complained. For the consequences of negligent misfeasance all could obtain redress. " But if a person asked a visitor to sleep at his house and the former failed to see that the sheets were properly aired and the visitor caught cold, he could maintain no action for there was no act of commission but simply an omission." For ten years judicial opinion oscillated between these alternatives, and, when the question was ripe for solution, Mr. Justice Willes seized his opportunity. In two masterly judgments in *Indermaur* v. *Dames* and *Gautret* v. *Egerton* he reviewed the cases, chose as the decisive test the character of the entrant and stated the principles which for ninety years his successors were content to accept.[7]

These cases now belong to history, but they afford an illuminating essay in judicial mechanics. The English judge, when he makes law in the fullest sense open to him, is, like all great artists, not so much an

---

[7] *Indermaur* v. *Dames* (1866) L.R. 1 C.P. 274 ; *Gautret* v. *Egerton* (1867) L.R. 2 C.P. 371.

innovator as an interpreter. He is necessarily conditioned by the material fortuitously given to him, by the anxiety not to impair judicial consistency and by the predominant feeling of the profession. Working within these limits, he transmutes experience into law and, by generalising, performs a genuine act of creation. Among such creators Willes stands supreme, and in the context of occupiers' liability he justified and crowned the experiments of his colleagues.

In the rich period of judicial activity between 1852 and 1875 individual duties of care had thus been established. The more generous approach to the law which the Judicature Acts seemed to invite suggested to eager or impatient minds the possiblity of enclosing them within a single comprehensive formula. The opportunity was offered in 1883 by the case of *Heaven* v. *Pender*.[8] The defendant owned a dry dock where ships might be repaired. For this purpose he erected a staging which, through his negligence, was unsafe. The plaintiff, a workman in the employ of a firm engaged to paint a ship in the dock, was injured when the staging collapsed. The Court of Appeal allowed him to recover damages. Lord Justice Cotton and Lord Justice Bowen were content to apply the analogy of *Indermaur* v. *Dames*. Lord Justice Brett was more audacious. After enumerating a number of specific duties, he embarked upon a scholastic exercise. " The logic of inductive reasoning requires that, where two major propositions lead to exactly similar minor premises, there must be a more remote and larger premise which embraces both of the major propositions."

[8] (1883) 11 Q.B.D. 503.

Thus fortified, he drew his conclusion. " The proposition which the recognised cases suggest, and which is therefore to be deduced from them, is that whenever one person is by circumstances placed in such a position with regard to another that everyone of ordinary sense who did think would at once recognise that if he did not use ordinary care and skill in his own conduct with regard to those circumstances he would cause danger of injury to the person or property of the other, a duty arises to use ordinary care and skill to avoid such danger." The duty of care, in short, was to be generalised on the basis of reasonable foresight.

In this case Lord Justice Brett, though bolder than his colleagues, at least agreed with their decision. In *Thomas* v. *Quartermaine* in 1887 [9] he found himself alone. The *ratio decidendi* turned upon the maxim *volenti non fit injuria*, but all three judges paused to discuss the more seductive question of duty. Brett, now Lord Esher, repeated his generalisation. Lord Justice Bowen emphatically rejected it. The duty of care did not exist " in the air "; it was a duty owed only " towards particular people." By this time the profession had digested Lord Esher's words and pondered their consequences, and it was clear that he was on a frolic of his own. Six years later in *Le Lièvre* v. *Gould* [10] he recanted. The case itself raised the peculiar question of negligent statements as opposed to acts, a situation outside the literal application of the formula in *Heaven* v. *Pender* and already covered

[9] (1887) 18 Q.B.D. 685.
[10] [1893] 1 Q.B. 491.

by adverse authority.[11] But Lord Esher's retreat was unequivocal. All that *Heaven* v. *Pender* had established was that "under certain circumstances one man may owe a duty to another even though there is no contract between them."

The preference of the common law for a catalogue of duties was emphasised by the appearance in 1889 of Beven's *Principles of the Law of Negligence*. In his preface the author remarked the recent and rapid development of his subject and the multiplicity of cases which he proposed "not merely to collect but to discuss"—a promise that he kept with formidable fidelity through twelve hundred pages of text. The book was published after *Heaven* v. *Pender* and *Thomas* v. *Quartermaine* but before *Le Lièvre* v. *Gould*, and Beven's reception of Lord Esher's experiment was ominous. It was "of such wide-spreading influence that a thorough examination of it was the only alternative to submissive adoption." It enjoyed, indeed, the support of several American authorities, and Beven was prepared to give "at least as much weight to a decision of the Supreme Court of the United States as to a decision of that fluid tribunal, a Divisional Court." [12] But a proposition suited to the wide spaces

---

[11] *Dickson* v. *Reuter's Telegram Co.* (1877) 3 C.P.D. 1. Lord Esher had here been a party to the decision in favour of the defendants.

[12] Much of the American influence in the last third of the nineteenth century was due to the appearance at the English Bar of the remarkable lawyer, Judah P. Benjamin. Secretary of State in the Confederate Government, he came to England when the Southern cause was lost and quickly became the foremost counsel in commercial cases. *Benjamin on Sale*, first published in 1868, remains a standard work. See Goodhart, *Five Jewish Lawyers of the Common Law*; Witt, *Life in the Law*, 158–168.

of the American continent might well be too broad
for the narrower needs of English litigants; and Beven
ended by rejecting the concept of a general duty and
compiling in its place a list of fifty-six separate duties.

This particular group of cases, while they reveal
the distrust of premature rationalisation, possess a
second and more individual interest. The judgments
reflected the opposing personalities of their authors.
A once fashionable school of jurists sought to explain
the mutations of the law in terms of human psychology.
From this dubious incursion into the underworld
there has since been a reaction. But, while the play
of judicial temperament is not to be exaggerated, it
may not be ignored. In the conflict between General
Duty and Specific Duties the protagonists were sharply
contrasted. Brett—vivid, impulsive, coarse of fibre,
impatient of subtlety—confronted Bowen, the scholar
in practice, precise, scrupulous, even fastidious, in the
spoken and in the written word. These qualities
coloured their views upon the function and value of
the jury. To Brett it was the body of good neighbours
whose standards the law should sanction. Bowen,
while not disdaining the raw material it offered, felt
the need to temper and polish it before it could be
made fit for expert use. Brett, though twenty years
the senior in age, outlived Bowen on the Bench, and
his valediction was both generous and candid. " His
reasoning," he said, " was so extremely accurate and
so beautifully fine that what he said sometimes escaped
my mind, which is not so finely edged." [13]

[13] William Baliol Brett (1815–99), as befitted a Cambridge
rowing Blue, is said by his biographer in the D.N.B. to have

Negligence, if the central, is not the only facet of civil liability. History or policy may require a legal system to impose, in special circumstances, a duty to insure persons against loss or injury. Between 1862 and 1868 attention was focused upon this need by the protracted litigation in *Rylands* v. *Fletcher*. To recapitulate the facts would be tedious, but the course of the action is not without interest.[14] It started life at the Liverpool Summer Assizes. The plaintiff obtained a verdict subject to the award of an arbitrator who was empowered to state a case for the opinion of the court. So singular an expedient measured the distance already travelled from the forms of action and challenged forensic ingenuity. When the case came before the Court of Exchequer, counsel for the plaintiff found it difficult to sustain a consistent argument. He offered a variety of dicta from the reports of two centuries, flanked by citations from *Gale on Easements* and Broom's *Legal Maxims*; but he relied more confidently upon the recent judgment of Mr. Justice Blackburn in *Williams* v. *Groucett*.[15] The plaintiff in this case was a farmer and the defendants owned the minerals beneath the surface of his land. In order to work them, they sank a shaft the mouth

showed at an early stage in his career " an unusual aptitude for marine cases." His practice, however, was wide and varied, and his appointment in 1868 as a judge of the Common Pleas was expected. He became a Lord Justice of Appeal in 1876 and, as Lord Esher, was Master of the Rolls from 1883 to 1897. According to his biographer, " his robust common sense, which predisposed him to make short work of technicalities, was united with a criterion of justice which was unduly elastic."

[14] It is to be traced in (1864) 3 H. & C. 774; (1866) L.R. 1 Ex. 265; (1868) L.R. 3 H.L. 330.   [15] (1863) 4 B. & S. 149.

of which they failed to fence. The plaintiff's mare
fell down it and was killed. Mr. Justice Blackburn
allowed the action. " When a party," he said, " alters
things from their normal condition so as to render
them dangerous to already acquired rights, the law
casts on him the obligation of fencing the danger so
that it shall not be injurious to those rights." Though
these words were prophetic, the case itself was not in
point; and Mellish, arguing for the defendants in
Rylands v. *Fletcher*, observed that the situation with
which the court had now to cope was unique. He
then formulated the issue with the instinctive grasp
of principle which later made him so sound a judge.[16]
Each party was engaged on his own land upon operations
in themselves lawful. The defendants had no reason
to anticipate danger to the plaintiff. The common
law imposed liability without negligence only in such
exceptional instances as those of common carriers
and innkeepers, and to these the present facts offered
no analogy. The court, by a majority, dismissed
the action. Baron Martin accepted Mellish's argument
and Chief Baron Pollock sought the easy refuge of
passivity. In the absence of authority " the safer
course is to decide in favour of the defendants." Baron
Bramwell dissented, partly on the doubtful ground
that the defendants were as much trespassers " as if
they had directly poured the water on to the plaintiff's
works," and more plausibly by insisting that the escape
of the water constituted a nuisance.

[16] " It was said of the late Lord Justice Mellish by Lord Cairns
that he went right instinctively: that is, he did not flounder
into truth." Birrell, *Res Judicatae*, 272.

The plaintiff appealed successfully to the Exchequer Chamber, and the judgment of a strong court, which included Willes, was delivered by Blackburn. After reviewing the facts and stating the problem, he enunciated the " true rule of law " in words which, though they have since become dangerously familiar, still spell riddles that await answers. " The person who for his own purposes brings on his lands and collects and keeps there anything likely to do mischief if it escapes must keep it in at his peril, and, if he does not do so, is *prima facie* answerable for all the damage which is the natural consequence of its escape." He fortified his rule with recollections of cattle trespass, dangerous animals and the more curious aspects of nuisance, but strangely forbore to repeat his own dictum from *Williams* v. *Groucett*. In the House of Lords only two judgments were delivered. Lord Cairns did little but affirm the propriety of Blackburn's exposition and Lord Cranworth said even less more feebly.

It is instructive to compare Blackburn's judgment in *Rylands* v. *Fletcher* with that of Willes in *Indermaur* v. *Dames*. Both judges accepted the unusual risk of formulating a general principle, a bold act more characteristic of Willes than of Blackburn. Each judgment was at once recognised as of major importance, and each has since been scrutinised as severely as though it had been the section of a statute. But the contrasts are as striking as the similarities. The language of *Indermaur* v. *Dames* is studied, simple and clear. It has been darkened only by the refinements of later judges. Instead of applying the master's words to the exigencies of each case—a process that he himself

had carefully prepared—they fell into the temptation
of translating questions of fact into propositions of
law and, by elaborating distinctions, overlaid the
original text with a crust of technical *minutiae*.
Blackburn's formula in *Rylands* v. *Fletcher* contained
within itself the seeds of controversy. Like all the
judges in the case, he assumed that, if the defendants
without fault on their part were to be held liable, such
severity required a special justification, and he would
seem to have found it in the unusual character of the
operation: some abnormality, as he expressed it in
his earlier case, some addition to the daily hazards
of life. But in his final summary he chose to speak
of " things likely to do mischief if they escape." To
distinguish normal and abnormal activity is not easy,
even if it presents the problem, familiar to all lawyers,
of placing a particular case on one side or the other
of a particular line. But Blackburn made the task
unnecessarily hard by using a phrase that obscured his
meaning, and Lord Cairns added a further complication
by his reference to a " non-natural use of land."

Indermaur v. *Dames*, moreover, crowned a decade
of litigation. Willes had there to make his choice
between alternative grounds of decision; and, having
chosen, he re-stated the purport of a coherent series
of cases. He made new law by revealing what was
already latent in the earlier judgments. Blackburn
in *Rylands* v. *Fletcher* was a pioneer, and his appeal
to the past was but the impulse to clothe innovation
with the appearance of continuity. The essential
novelty of his rule was recognised at once by contemporaries, and later writers, when they sought to

" place " it in the development of the common law, went to extravagant lengths to supply it with a suitable background. Bohlen discussed it in terms of social conflict, and, while Pound exposed this fallacy, his own attempt to make a picture by fitting it into the mosaic of a " collectivist movement " seems no less fantastic.[17] It is certainly one of the functions of law to answer economic needs, and those needs will be most clearly articulated by such persons or bodies as can best afford the luxury of litigation. But to express law purely, or even primarily, in terms of economics is to betray obsession with an *idée fixe*.

It may finally be said of Blackburn in *Rylands* v. *Fletcher* that, while he accepted the occasional necessity of a sterner duty than that of care, neither he nor his colleagues supposed themselves to be solemnly creating a dual standard of civil liability. The rule, however fruitful it might prove to be, remained in some degree isolated in the general scheme of the common law. It is significant that in none of the arguments or judgments in the case was any attempt made to equate it with an important and well-established example of responsibility without fault—that involved in the relationship of master and servant.

The sporadic case law that had sufficed while this relationship was domestic was too feeble to withstand the irruption into trade and industry of the limited liability company. In the process of revaluation Willes and Blackburn were again conspicuous. Their methods appear in the case of *Limpus* v. *London General Omnibus*

---

[17] Bohlen, *Studies in the Law of Torts*, 344; Pound, *Interpretations of Legal History*, 105–109.

Company,[18] decided a few years before *Rylands* v. *Fletcher*. On the one hand they dismissed as irrelevant the servant's disobedience to his orders: " the law is not so futile as to allow the masters, by giving secret instructions to a servant, to set aside their liability." On the other hand they insisted that the servant should at least have intended to promote the master's interests and that he should have acted " within the scope of his employment." To this phrase, already trite, they gave a new significance and a wider currency; but, while they and their colleagues thus drew the outlines of a modern doctrine of Vicarious Liability,[19] they were so far from including it, together with the rule in *Rylands* v. *Fletcher*, in a single concept of strict obligation that they sought rather to excuse than to justify it. Many and specious were the judicial efforts at rationalisation. The master, though he had done no wrong, was liable because he had the power or duty of control, because it was he who profited by the service, because he should have been more careful in the choice of his subordinates.[20] Willes was strong enough to tell the truth. As a source of reparation, let alone of costs, the servant was a man of straw. " There should be some person capable of paying damages and who may be sued by people who are injured." [21]

---

[18] (1862) 1 H. & C. 526. See also *Barwick* v. *English Joint Stock Bank* (1867) L.R. 2 Ex. 259.

[19] The name itself seems to have been invented by Sir Frederick Pollock: see *Pollock–Holmes Letters*, I, 233.

[20] See *Duncan* v. *Findlater* (1839) 6 Cl. & F. 901: *Hall* v. *Smith* (1824) 2 Bing. 156: *Quarman* v. *Burnett* (1840) 6 M. & W. 499.

[21] *Limpus* v. *London General Omnibus Co.* (1862) 1 H. & C. 526, at p. 529.

It is fair to say that by the end of the century the judges had met the challenge of the new forces which, with bewildering speed and variety, pressed upon them during the long reign of Victoria. They had discerned their legal implications and had replaced the forms of action by a miscellany of torts. If they had remained obstinately pragmatic, they need not therefore be reproached. Meditation is not a chronic indulgence of Bench or Bar. If a legal philosopher be needed, he must be sought among the jurists.

In 1860 Addison published *Wrongs and their Remedies*. Though the sub-title was " A Treatise on the Law of Torts," he made no attempt to generalise. Plunging at once into " infringements upon territorial rights," he plodded doggedly over the difficult country opened up by the judges until he reached home with " matrimonial and parental injuries, adultery and seduction." Negligence he relegated to a companion volume on Contracts. As a digest for practitioners it succeeded: to jurisprudence it made no pretence. Pollock, in a review of the seventh edition, justly remarked that " it is as a hunting-ground for authority that the lawyer uses a textbook of this character." [22]

In the next twenty years two distinguished jurists, Sir William Markby in England and Oliver Wendell Holmes in the United States, examined the problem of civil liability as part of a more ambitious analysis of common law concepts. The first edition of Markby's *Elements of Law* appeared in 1871. [23] In the absence

[22] 9 L.Q.R. (1893), 321–322.
[23] Sir William Markby (1829–1914) took a first class in the Honours School of Mathematics at Oxford, was called to the Bar in 1856 and ten years later was made a judge of the High

of any definition of tort, the author felt that he " must turn to the actual practice of the law and see how judges do in fact deal with the question of liability," and he examined " the phrases in common use among lawyers when they wish to give their reasons why a duty exists in some cases and not in others." The field was not fertile; and, remarking the richness of the judicial language and the poverty of the judicial ideas, he was driven to conclude that " the reason why lawyers have shrunk from testing accurately the conventional phrases which they use about liability is that it lays too bare the truth that the nature of many primary duties is only determined by reference to an imaginary standard." Law, it might almost be supposed, is what the jury thinks. Twenty-five years later, in his fifth edition, he had still to admit failure in the search for principle.[24] He noticed, indeed, " a disposition to make blameworthiness the connecting link between acts which are called torts," and he observed the special importance of negligence where reproach was always seasonable. He even toyed with the notion of confining the scope of tort to the breach of a duty of care. Within this restricted area symmetry might doubtless be imposed upon the law. But the definition was arbitrary and left outside, unclassified and disconsolate, not

Court of Bengal. He remained for twelve years in India and combined with judicial office the Vice-Chancellorship of the University of Calcutta. In 1878 he was persuaded by Dr. Jowett to become the first Reader in Indian Law in Oxford and held the Readership until 1900. Beside his *Elements of Law*, he lectured and wrote on Indian Law; and, as a young man, he had helped Mrs. Austin to prepare her husband's posthumous works.

[24] *Elements of Law*, 5th ed. (1896), Chap. XVI.

only the instances of strict liability but such familiar actions as those for deceit and defamation. Markby offered a counsel of despair; and it was the more desperate that he was compelled to dismiss, as a gallant failure, Lord Esher's attempt to generalise even the central duty of care.

Unlike Markby, Holmes was able to make the most of the two worlds he had conquered. If in the study he was tempted to soar too far from the ground, in the court he was soon brought back to earth. As a jurist he was not enamoured of the speculative judge. " I am afraid," he wrote to Pollock, " you would think me arrogant if I should say how little importance I attach to the discussions of the run of judges, whether English or American, on matters involving general theory." [25] As a judge he was himself regarded with suspicion by " mere lawyers." When he was translated from Massachussets to the Supreme Court of the United States, the *New York Evening Post* described him as " more of a ' literary feller ' than one often finds on the bench with a strong tendency to be brilliant rather than sound." [26] " Literary " and " judicial," " brilliant " and " sound "—these antitheses are still felt to be inevitable and fatal. But in retrospect it may be said of Holmes, as he said of Maine, that " he had the gift of imparting a ferment which is one of the marks of genius." [27]

In the third and fourth of his lectures on *The Common Law* he set himself to discover, if this were at all possible, a single root of civil liability. The quest, he admitted,

[25] *Pollock–Holmes Letters*, I, 65.
[26] *Pollock–Holmes Letters*, I, 103–104.   [27] *Ibid.*, I, 31.

was dark and doubtful. The law began with no premise and any conclusion had to be drawn, or fabricated, from the accidents and effects of litigation. But it accorded with the " philosophical habit of the day " to which even judges had succumbed [28]; and Holmes was the child of his time and the son of his father. As a moralist he was loth to divorce law from ethics. As a scientist he longed to probe to the heart of the judgments where, if anywhere, principle lay concealed and which were spread before him as so many subjects for dissection. The vocabulary of torts abounded with moral phraseology, but the content of the phrases was slight. No court could be concerned with the personal culpability of a defendant. All conduct must be reduced to an external standard and tested by its reaction upon the jury—in Holmes' flattering tribute, upon the " ideal, average, prudent man." So far he agreed with Markby. But he was not content to leave everything to the jury. Verdicts offered judges the chance and the means of constructing concrete rules, and it was by this regular transmutation from fact to law that the volume of Torts was compiled. Words so distinct in apparent connotation as " negligence " and " intent " suffered the same metamorphosis. Even in so flagrant a case as deceit the common law, " starting from the moral ground," had worked out " an external standard of what would be fraudulent in the average prudent member of the community " which all at their peril must avoid. His conclusion is best summarised in a letter to Pollock. " The general

---

[28] To this tendency, it must be allowed, most English judges had offered a stout resistance.

criterion in tort is the tendency of an act under the circumstances known to the actor according to human experience. If the probability of harm is great and manifest, the act is called malicious or intentional. If less, but still sufficient to impose liability, it is called negligent." [29]

The publication of his lectures had an immediate effect upon all writers on the common law in England no less than in the United States, and the echoes were heard even in the dim recesses of the Oxford and Cambridge Schools. " Nemesis is upon us," Pollock reported in 1893. " The reasonable man and the external standard have filtered down to the common examination candidate, who is beginning to write horrible nonsense about them." [30] But, while so acid a test of civil liability might be defended as a laboratory exercise, it was at once too nice and too remote for the judge grappling with the infinite diversity of facts. He, for his part, could not afford so relentless an analysis. He had to satisfy coarser instincts and at least to act as if such words as " intent " and " negligence " had different meanings. Holmes himself knew better than to practise as a judge what he preached as a jurist. Apophthegms that adorned the professor at the breakfast table were unseemly and impracticable in court. [31] Nor in truth did he find it easy to reduce to his single criterion either the rule in *Rylands* v. *Fletcher* or the

[29] *Pollock–Holmes Letters*, I, 35–36.
[30] *Ibid.*, I, 46.
[31] When he occasionally succumbed to the temptation to " air his views " in a judgment, he found it advisable, after consulting his colleagues, to " cut down the discussion ": *Pollock–Holmes Letters*, I, 35.

doctrine of vicarious liability. The former must be
received as an act of policy. Where there was an
added element of danger, "the safest way to secure
care is to throw the risk upon the person who decides
what precautions shall be taken."[32] To explain the
latter he was driven to a fanciful relict of Roman slavery.
Of this aberration it is enough to say with Pollock and
Maitland that "any theory that would connect our
'employer's liability' with slavery has before it a
difficult task." [33]

In 1887 Pollock published the first English book
devoted to a scholarly and systematic examination of
torts. He described it as "a treatise on the principles
of obligations arising from civil wrongs in the common
law," and he prefaced it with a tribute to Holmes in
particular and to the Harvard Law School in general.
His purpose was to show "that there really is a Law of
Tort and not merely a number of rules about various
kinds of torts." How he fared upon his pilgrimage
may best be seen not from the first edition but from
the sixth, written in the last year of Victoria's reign.
He proclaimed at the outset "a broad principle,"
which he found in the "general duty owed by all
members of a civilised commonwealth towards their
neighbours to do them no hurt without lawful cause
or excuse." The most devoted research, he admitted,
could trace no such duty in the authorities; and he
was forced to pray in aid Ulpian and the Catechism
of the Anglican Church wherein the catechumen

[32] *The Common Law*, 116–117.
[33] *Ibid.*, Lecture I; Pollock and Maitland, *Hist. of Eng. Law*, II,
528.

undertook " to hurt nobody by word nor deed, to be true and just in all his dealings." With such remote guarantors, it is not surprising that, having stated his principle, Pollock proceeded at once to abandon it. He substituted a triple classification of torts known to the common law.

In the first group were " personal wrongs." Here the conduct of the defendant was " wilful or wanton " and the moral content strong.[34] In the second were " wrongs to possession and property." Here the ethical element seemed conspicuously absent, and Pollock sought consolation in history. These wrongs were *disjecta membra* from the law of property, transformed through preoccupation with the forms of action to the law of torts where they survived, atavistic and unassimilated intruders. But he was not content to explain: he sought to justify or at least to excuse. " It may seem unreasonable at first sight to expect a man to know at his peril what things are his neighbour's. But it is not evidently unreasonable to expect him to know what is his own, and this is only the statement of the same rule from the other side." The plea of mitigation is unconvincing. The typical tort of this group is conversion, and the typical case of conversion is the contest between two innocent victims of an unsuspected fraud. It is precisely because each has good grounds for claiming a thing as his own that the action is fought. The third group comprised " wrongs to person, estate and property generally,"

---

[34] Not until nine years later did the House of Lords decide *Hulton* v. *Jones* [1910] A.C. 20, and it is not surprising that Pollock then attacked it bitterly. See *Pollock–Holmes Letters*, I, 156 and 26 L.Q.R. 103.

a clumsy title devised to embrace such torts as negligence
and nuisance. These had " a kind of intermediate
character." They were " not as a rule wilfully or
wantonly harmful, but neither were they morally
indifferent."

Faced with this classification, Pollock, like a kindly
surgeon, proposed to amputate the second group of
wrongs. If these could be restored to the law of
property, where by history and context they belonged,
a residuary body of civil liability would be left secure
upon an ethical basis. But, even were the operation
practicable, the patient would not emerge immaculate.
With Pollock, as with Holmes, two eccentricities
obstinately defied discipline. The rule in *Rylands* v.
Fletcher, though included in the third group, lacked
the element of negligence that marked and reconciled
its fellow members. Pollock could only accept and
deplore a *res judicata*. " How far such a rule can be
theoretically or historically justified is not an open
question for English courts of justice, for it has been
explicitly affirmed by the House of Lords." The doctrine
of Vicarious Liability was still more refractory. To
the jurist even more painfully than to the judge, it was
inartistic to repose on the sordid ground of expediency.[35]
Pollock for a time was driven desperately to suggest
that it was hazardous to embark upon business at all [36]:
a servant was almost a *Rylands* v. *Fletcher* object.
But by the date of his sixth edition he had ceased to

---

[35] Maitland hinted at the shameful truth. " Should we nowadays
hold masters answerable for the uncommanded torts of their
servants if normally servants were able to pay for the damage
they do ? " (*Hist. of Eng. Law*, II, 532).

[36] *Essays in Jurisprudence and Ethics*, 125.

kick against the pricks and, resigned if not persuaded, he left the doctrine to speak for itself.

Pollock was much too formidable a personality to be criticised in his lifetime with impunity and too considerable a figure in professional literature to be dismissed posthumously as an Eminent Victorian. But even his tough mind was enervated by the contemporary itch to moralise; and it is not surprising that few of his colleagues escaped infection. Ames in the United States, after an imaginative reconstruction of " early law," reflected with modest complacency that " the ethical standard of reasonable conduct had replaced the unmoral standard of acting at one's peril." [37] In England Kenny, noting the case of *Stanley* v. *Powell*,[38] marked " the change which had passed over the conception of the legal liability for tort. The older decisions paid more regard to the fact that the plaintiff had sustained a loss through the defendant's conduct than to the question whether there was anything in that conduct so blameworthy as to justify them in shifting this loss from one man's shoulders to another's." Today, he was happy to report, " the idea of culpability had become judicially associated with that of liability for torts." He had only to regret that the recent Workmen's Compensation Act had " indicated a reversion on the part of the legislature to the older and cruder view." If Parliament had

---

[37] *Law and Morals*, included in *Lectures on Legal History* at p. 437.

[38] *Cases on the Law of Torts*, 146. Though the book was not published until 1904, it represented, as Kenny explained in the preface, the results of an annual course of lectures over the ten preceding years.

been content to leave law-making to the courts, the progressive man could have slept soundly in his chambers or his study.

In the result the jurists were not more successful than the judges in their attempts to generalise civil liability. It may be thought, indeed, that the judges were not only, as was to be expected, more prudent but more sensible. While they inevitably shared the ethical bias of their age, they did not feel impelled at all hazards to equate moral and legal obligation and they were not unduly alarmed if the two seemed at times to diverge. If it were convenient to impose liability without fault, they bowed to the necessity. Why should there not be more than one standard of conduct ? The reader of Pollock's pages is tempted to recall a snatch of dialogue from Henry James.[39]

" He makes it, somehow, such a grand, possible affair."

" Ah well, if he makes it possible."

" I mean especially he makes it grand."

Pollock's proposals are grand enough, but they are scarcely possible. Faced with the fragments of life, the current law of any place and time can but approximate to a principle or indicate a tendency. Looking back upon the individual torts as they had emerged at the end of the nineteenth century, it requires an act of faith to postulate that principle or to indicate the goal to which they were tending.

---

[39] *The Wings of the Dove.*

CHAPTER 3

CORPORATE PERSONALITY

THE immense and at times feverish activity of the nineteenth century offered opportunities and involved risks too great to be compassed by individual enterprise. Nor could the speed and flexibility that the new conditions demanded be satisfied by the cumbrous dignity of the common law corporation. The need was met by the joint stock company created under the authority either of a special or of a general Act of Parliament. The pioneers were the railways, and their adventures in the early years of Victoria's reign tell a sufficient story.[1]

In 1837 fifty railway companies were operating under thirty Acts over five hundred miles of track. Human freight was subsidiary to the carriage of goods and passengers were herded in trucks at the end of coal trains. A depression between 1840 and 1843 was followed, as the classical economists prescribed, by a boom. In 1845 two hundred railway Bills were presented to Parliament, three thousand miles of new line were constructed, a Great Western train reached the speed of forty-four miles an hour on the journey from Paddington to Bristol and a thrilling series of accidents attested the marvels of mechanical science. The " railway mania " culminated in 1846, when

[1] For a full and fascinating account, see Lewin, *Early British Railways*.

two hundred and seventy Bills received the Royal
Assent and provided for new construction at a cost of
£350,000,000. But by 1847 the boom was over. A
disastrous financial crisis broke many firms of the
highest credit and of all kinds, the Bank Act had to
be relaxed and pending railway schemes postponed or
abandoned.

The fluctuating fortunes of the railways during
this decade, if sensational, were not singular. All
manner of companies were being incorporated by
special Act of Parliament for all manner of projects.
But in the first twenty-five years of the reign four
Acts were passed of general application and importance.[2]
The first, in 1844, was fashioned on the familiar model
of the conveyancers.[3] It provided for a Deed of
Settlement where the purpose of the company was to
be stated and the lines drawn within which the directors
were to act, though the Deed itself might be altered
by subsequent resolution. The shareholders were as
yet personally liable for the company's debts; but a
second Act of 1855 introduced the principle of limited
liability. In 1856 the pattern of conveyancing was
abandoned and the Deed of Settlement split into two
parts: a Memorandum of Association and the Articles
of Association.[4] At length in 1862 the first great
Companies Act was passed. This Act required the
objects of a company to be set out in the Memorandum
and expressly forbade any alteration. It was designed

[2] See Horrwitz, "Company Law Reform and the Ultra Vires
Doctrine," 62 L.Q.R. 66.
[3] Joint Stock Companies Act, 1844.
[4] Limited Liability Act, 1855, and Joint Stock Companies Act,
1856.

presumably to protect creditors who might now be exposed to the recklessness of shareholders no longer inhibited by the fear of individual responsibility, but it applied alike to limited and to unlimited companies.

The new economy thus sanctioned embraced and challenged so many interests that the resources of the current law must have seemed doubtfully adequate for their adjustment. Providentially litigation was abundant, and the judges were afforded ample occasion to exercise their ingenuity. Their reaction may be observed both in contract and in tort.

In 1846 the case of *Coleman* v. *Eastern Counties Railway Company* came before the Master of the Rolls, Lord Langdale.[5] The company had been authorised to build and maintain a railway between London and Harwich, and the directors now proposed to promote a steam-packet service from Harwich to the Continent. A shareholder sought an injunction to restrain this extravagance. Lord Langdale, the friend of Austin and the disciple of Bentham, ardent reformer not only of Chancery process but of the Public Records and of the British Museum, was not the man to wait upon precedent. He accepted the novelty of the case and summoned his resources to meet it. " Companies of this kind, possessing most extensive powers, have so recently been introduced into this country that neither the legislature nor the courts have yet been able to understand all the different lights in which their transactions ought to be viewed." The field of operations was too vast to be covered by the law of partnership, and the only solution was to interpret the

[5] (1846) 10 Beav. 1.

statute under which the company purported to act. Policy, moreover, required a strict interpretation. The court must protect both the public, who might otherwise be ravaged by the monsters they had created, and the shareholders who had risked their money on the faith of the invitation made to them. The latter were, if necessary, to be saved from themselves and weaned from the " wild speculation " excited by the " frenzy of the last fifteen years." If, therefore, the proposal in question was not precisely within the powers conferred by the parent Act, even the acquiescence of the shareholders could not make it valid. Lord Langdale, in effect, approached the whole question from the angle of an equity judge who must guard the beneficiaries from the greed or corruption of the trustees, and he had no scruple in granting an injunction to restrain a threatened breach of trust.

The implications of the joint stock company, thus exposed, were analysed in a series of judgments by Baron Parke. He was seen here at his best—clear, decisive, practical; and a case of 1853 is a fair specimen of his technique. Two railway companies had made a contract whereby the one obtained the right, on the payment of tolls, to use the other's lines. When disputes arose the defendant company pleaded that the contract was *ultra vires*.[6] The question, said Parke, " though one of great importance and some nicety, lies in a narrow compass and depends upon the construction of

---

[6] *South Yorks. Ry.* v. *G.N. Ry.* (1853) 9 Ex. 55. The phrase *ultra vires* was already familiar in this context, and in *Royal British Bank* v. *Turquand* (1855) 5 E. & B. 248 Willes *arguendo* could speak of " what has been called the *ultra vires* doctrine."

the Railway Clauses Consolidation Act, 1845." A corporation, itself the " creature of law," might, no more than an individual, treat a promise with levity. But, where it was created by Parliament for particular purposes and with special powers, it could not be bound by any contract into which it had assumed to enter unless the authority to make it was given, expressly or by necessary inference, by its Act. That the question was one of statutory interpretation was agreed by all the members of the court. Like all such questions, however, it admitted of more than one answer and the choice was one of policy. Baron Martin read the relevant words with careful severity. He thought the alleged contract " highly objectionable " and wished to annul a transaction which tempted the directors to " traffick in shares " and was " most pernicious to the shareholders."[7] Parke, with whom Baron Platt agreed, gave the words a generous meaning and saved the company from dishonour. He was " happy to find that the law of this case coincides with the honesty of it and does not sanction the breach by the defendants of the solemn contract into which they have fairly entered and from which they are trying to escape." Chief Baron Pollock, who disliked Parke and was Baron Martin's father-in-law, grudgingly decided " not to dissent from the majority." Four years later in

[7] Baron Martin, though he thus set his face against commercial speculation, was not averse from its counterpart on the turf. He was " an excellent judge of horseflesh " (D.N.B.). This, however, sufficed for his recreation. Literature, in particular, he rarely sought outside the reports. He was once induced to read *Romeo and Juliet*, but found it " just a tissue of improbabilities from beginning to end " (E. Bowen-Rowlands, *Seventy-two Years at the Bar*, 76.)

Ernest v. *Nicholls*,[8] a case involving two insurance companies, Parke felt able to say that " the principles upon which the liability of joint stock companies is to be decided . . . are clear and perfectly settled," though, he was driven to add, " they are not always in practice kept steadily in view." All turned upon the language of the statute. If it could be read so as to uphold the contract and preserve commercial probity, this should be done. If the language were too peremptory and too unambiguous to allow this construction, the contract must be avoided. Nor, indeed, was such a result necessarily harsh or improper. The legislature had provided sufficient publicity for the area of a company's activities to be widely known. If persons " do not choose to acquaint themselves with the powers of the directors, it is their own fault."

Baron Parke was too sanguine. With the passing of the Companies Act, 1862, the settlement he had envisaged was disturbed by an unhappy recourse to the concepts of partnership and agency which both he and Lord Langdale had rejected. The digression was the more alarming since it was sanctioned by the great names of Willes and Blackburn.[9]

In 1871 a company incorporated under the Companies Act had made a contract which was undoubtedly *ultra vires* but which the shareholders had purported to ratify. Mr. Justice Willes accepted as axiomatic the application of the normal rules of agency and upheld the contract. " The law with regard to ratification is

---

[8] (1857) 6 H.L.C. 401.

[9] Lindley, by calling his book a *Treatise on the Law of Partnership, including its application to Companies*, had encouraged this error: *supra*, p. 18.

clear. . . . The principle, by which a person on whose behalf an act is done without his authority may ratify and adopt it, is as old as any proposition known to the law." [10] The implications of this assumption were large. If it were proper to apply the doctrine of ratification, the shareholders must be identified with the company: corporation and members must be a single entity. So drastic a conclusion invited criticism, and in 1874 and 1875 the whole question was examined afresh in the great case of *Riche* v. *Ashbury Railway Carriage Co.*[11]

The defendant company was incorporated under the Companies Act, 1862. By the memorandum of association its objects were to traffic in all manner of railway machinery and rolling stock, to conduct the business of engineers, to work mines and to sell merchants' materials. Seeking still wider scope for their enterprise, the directors contracted on behalf of the company to build a railway in Belgium and made a further contract with the plaintiff to employ him in the construction of this line. After he had done some work and received some payment, the defendants asserted that his contract was *ultra vires* and stopped the work on which he was engaged. He claimed damages for breach of contract. The Barons of the Exchequer all agreed that the contract was *ultra vires* but that ratification was possible. The question was whether it had indeed been ratified; and, while Baron Bramwell differed on the facts, the majority thought that it had. They followed Willes in applying the

[10] *Phosphate of Lime Co.* v. *Green* (1871) L.R. 7 C.P. 43.
[11] (1874) L.R. 9 Ex. 224, 249; (1875) L.R. 7 H.L. 653.

common law rules of agency and felt no compunction in identifying the corporation with its members. The shareholders, in the words of Baron Channell, " constituted the company." On appeal the Exchequer Chamber was equally divided. Three judges held that an *ultra vires* contract was incapable of ratification and three that it could be and had been ratified. Among the latter was Blackburn. He saw no impropriety in applying to a company the normal rules both of partnership and of agency. Nor did he think that the Companies Act had made any difference. A corporation, whatever its nature or origin, must be bound, like an individual, by the decent and familiar maxims of the common law.

The House of Lords repelled these heresies and restored the pure process of interpretation initiated by Baron Parke. Lord Cairns was severe upon his colleagues in the courts below. " The history and progress of the action were not creditable to our legal proceedings." The case itself was of an " extremely simple character " and had been obscured and protracted solely through the incomprehension of the judges. They had misunderstood both the purpose and the effect of the Companies Act, whose design was to protect not only the shareholders but also the public and in particular the creditors of a company. It had therefore confined the scope of corporate activities to the range indicated by the memorandum of association. It was the task of the judges to interpret that memorandum and the words of the Act in the light of the facts. Different constructions were certainly possible; but, if the court concluded that a purported contract was *ultra vires*, it was void *ab initio*, and no efforts of the shareholders, however strenuous, could make the unborn live. " If every shareholder had been in the room and every shareholder had said, ' That is a contract which we desire to make, which we authorise the directors to make, to which we sanction the placing of the seal of the company,' the case would not have stood in any different position from that in which it stands now. The shareholders would thereby, by unanimous consent, have been attempting to do the very thing which, by Act of Parliament, they were prohibited from doing."

The true faith had been proclaimed *ex cathedra*, and it was only thereafter to be disturbed by the qualms momentarily induced by the manoeuvres of the " one-man company." This curious creature was so disliked by some judges that they were ready to strain the process of interpretation if they might thus prevent sharp practice. They were exercised between 1895 and 1897 by the ingenious activities of Aron Salomon, a bootmaker.[12] To convert his personal business into one of limited liability he registered a company under the Act of 1862; and, to satisfy the required minimum of seven shareholders, he took himself twenty thousand shares and gave one each to his wife, his daughter and his four sons. After a short and fitful life the company was wound up, and the question was whether, as against the outside creditors, the bootmaker and itself were distinct legal personalities.

Mr. Justice Vaughan Williams and the Court of

[12] *Broderip* v. *Salomon* [1895] 2 Ch. 323; *Salomon* v. *Salomon & Co.* [1897] A.C. 22.

Appeal held that the company must be identified with the man. Lord Lindley, indulging a sentimentality scarce worthy of one who had aspired to analytical jurisprudence, denounced it as " created for an illegitimate purpose ": though in form a separate person, it was in truth but " a device to defraud creditors." But once more the House of Lords recalled the judges to the straight and narrow path. The course of the law was not to be diverted at the suspicion of misconduct. The one clear principle, never to be forsaken, was the status of the corporation as a legal entity distinct from its shareholders, be they few or many. " It has become the fashion," said Lord Macnaghten, " to call companies of this class ' one-man companies.' That is a taking nickname, but it does not help one much in the way of argument. If it is intended to convey the meaning that a company which is under the absolute control of one person is not a company legally incorporated, although the requirements of the Act of 1862 may have been complied with, it is inaccurate and misleading. If it merely means that there is a predominant partner possessing an overwhelming influence and entitled practically to the whole of the profits, there is nothing in that contrary to the true intention of the Act or against public policy or detrimental to the interests of the creditors. If the shares are fully paid up, it cannot matter whether they are in the hands of one or many. If the shares are not fully paid, it is as easy to gauge the solvency of an individual as to estimate the financial ability of a crowd." Lord Halsbury concurred with characteristic vigour. " Either the limited company was a legal entity or it was not. If it was, the business belonged to it and not to Mr. Salomon. If it was not, there was no person and no thing to be an agent at all. It is impossible to say at the same time that there is a company and that there is not."

While the judges were thus striving to delimit the contractual capacity of a corporation, they had simultaneously to set it within the framework of civil liability. By the accession of Queen Victoria it was accepted in principle that a corporation might be sued for a tort committed by its servants.[13] It was indeed the advent of the joint-stock company that had accentuated the doctrine of vicarious liability. The crucial question in every case was whether the servant, when he committed the tort, was acting with the authority of the corporation. Here as elsewhere it was the ubiquity of the railways that supplied the judges with the material of decision.

In 1851 the servant of a railway company arrested a passenger for the alleged breach of a by-law. The passenger sued the company for assault and obtained a verdict. In the Exchequer Chamber Willes for the company offered a curious assortment of arguments.[14] A corporation could not be sued for trespass to the person: it had power to deal with property but none to commit assault. For this proposition he was driven to retreat upon his peculiar knowledge of the Year Books. If, on the other hand, a railway company were immune from medieval precept and might in exceptional circumstances be held liable for a personal

[13] See *Maund* v. *Monmouthshire Canal Co.* (1842) 4 M. & G. 452.
[14] *Eastern Counties Railway Co.* v. *Broom* (1851) 6 Ex. 314.

wrong, the authority to commit it must have been conferred under its common seal. An assault was "not an everyday act which a corporation may direct without the intervention of a solemn instrument." If, nevertheless, no deed were required, the tort could scarcely be assumed to benefit the company. It must therefore be ratified *ex post facto*, and no ratification emerged from the facts. Willes must surely have made his first two points with his tongue in his cheek; and Mr. Justice Patteson, who delivered the judgment of the Exchequer Chamber, was not the man to succumb to what, in any other counsel, must be described as sophistry.[15] Whatever the doctrine of the Year Books, contemporary society required, and contemporary law imposed, corporate liability for trespass to the person no less than to property, and to demand a deed was absurd. But Mr. Justice Patteson agreed that the servant must have been expressly authorised to commit the assault, and, as there had been no prior command, the plaintiff must prove a subsequent ratification. This he had failed to do; and on this ground, and this ground only, judgment was given for the company.

Ten years later the court was involved in the more intricate problem of implied authority. In *Goff* v.

[15] John Patteson was the son of a Suffolk clergyman and was educated at Eton and King's College, Cambridge. He was made a Judge of the King's Bench in 1830 at the age of 40 and after only nine years at the Bar. He at once made his mark as a judge. "No one," said Foss, "was more soundly versed in the principles of the common law or more lucid in his reasoning." Deafness enforced his premature retirement in 1852.

Great Northern Railway [16] the plaintiff had been arrested
by a ticket collector in the mistaken belief that he
had not paid his fare. The Railway Clauses Act, 1845,
imposed a penalty for travelling without payment
and empowered railway officials to take defaulters
into custody. Mr. Justice Blackburn delivered the
judgment of the Queen's Bench in the plaintiff's favour.
As the Act contemplated arrest in an appropriate
case, the collector must be taken to enjoy implied
authority to make it on an honest, if erroneous, view
of the facts. If the company's interests were to be
protected, time could not be afforded to consult the
directors, and subordinates must be allowed some
measure of initiative.

So far the courts had not been required to examine
in tort the complications introduced by the doctrine
of *ultra vires* with which they had become familiar
in contract. But they were faced with them in 1867
in *Poulton* v. *London and South-Western Railway
Company*,[17] a case which, though it has not caused
much uneasiness to later judges, has embarrassed the
more delicate minds of the jurists. Another passenger
had been arrested by another official, but this time
in the mistaken belief that he had not paid for the
carriage of his horse. The Act of 1845 met this emer-
gency by providing that the horse might be detained
but not the man. Once more, in the absence of an
express command, Mr. Justice Blackburn had to seek
implied authority; and the difference from *Goff* v.

[16] (1861) 3 E. & E. 672.
[17] (1867) L.R. 2 Q.B. 534. See also *Moore* v. *Metropolitan
Railway Co.* (1872) L.R. 8 Q.B. 36.

Great Northern Railway was immediately apparent.
In the new case the official had taken upon himself to
do an act which the corporation had no statutory power
to sanction: " a thing," said Blackburn, " which there
can be no possible ground for supposing the railway
company authorised him to do and which could never
be right on the part of the company to do." Mr.
Justice Mellor agreed. " I cannot think that it ever
can be implied that the company authorised the station-
master to do that which they have no authority to do
themselves."

In 1874 in the case of *Mill* v. *Hawker* [18] the doctrine
of *ultra vires* was canvassed in an unusual context.
The plaintiff had obstructed a path that crossed his
field and that was alleged to be a public highway. The
members of a Highway Board resolved at a formal
meeting that the obstruction should be removed, and
their surveyor, under their orders, removed it. The
plaintiff sued in trespass both the surveyor and the
members of the Board. No evidence was offered that
the path was in fact a public highway. Chief Baron
Kelly ordered the plaintiff to be non-suited. Neither
surveyor nor members could be held liable: the former
because, in executing his orders, he was protected
by the Highway Act, 1862, the latter because the action
should have been brought not against them but against
the Board itself. On further argument the Court of
Exchequer was divided. The Chief Baron still thought
he was right, but the majority granted a rule to set
aside the non-suit and obtain a new trial. The act
done was *ultra vires* the Board. It followed that the

[18] (1874) L.R. 9 Ex. 309; (1875) L.R. 10 Ex. 92.

surveyor was not protected by the Highway Act and
that the Board itself could not be sued despite the
resolution passed at the meeting. After this brave
attempt to solve the problem left open in *Poulton's*
case and to determine the effect of express authority
to do an *ultra vires* act, the judges lapsed into a *non
sequitur*. As the corporation escaped liability, this
must be cast upon the individual members. On appeal
to the Exchequer Chamber it was finally agreed that
the act done was *ultra vires* and that the surveyor could
therefore be sued. This conclusion sufficed to set
aside the non-suit, and the court would hazard no
further opinion. Mr. Justice Blackburn, who had
moved with confidence through the tangles of implied
authority, now drew back. It was unnecessary, and
therefore undesirable, to pronounce upon the liability
of the individual members. Judicial dissension was
not only unhelpful, it was undignified. " Our decision
would be of no assistance in sending the case down to
trial and would perhaps be an embarrassment to the
learned judge who may have to try it. We think it
better to leave the decision of the Court of Exchequer
. . . with the authority it had before, no better and
no worse." Whether the judges below were gratified
by this tribute to their learning is unreported. But
the prudence or timidity of the Exchequer Chamber
left uncertain the liability of a corporation for an
ultra vires tort committed by its servants and expressly
ordered by the resolution of its governing body. The
question is still unanswered.

Concentration upon the basic problem of authority
did not preclude an occasional and singular diversion.

In the few torts where motive and therefore malice were relevant, could inquiry be made into the sentiments of a corporation? This anthropomorphic curiosity intrigued the court in *Stevens* v. *Midland Railway*.[19] The plaintiff sued the defendants for malicious prosecution and failed because their servant had acted without authority. But it was argued that, even had the directors ordered the prosecution, the corporation, as it was incapable of malice, would have been likewise incapable of liability. Baron Alderson accepted the argument. " To support the action, it must be shown that the defendant was actuated by a motive in his mind, and a corporation has no mind." Four years later this dictum was used by counsel to submit that in libel malice was an essential ingredient and that therefore a corporation must be immune.[20] Lord Campbell dismissed the suggestion by recalling the distinction between " malice in law " and " malice in fact." " Malice in law " meant nothing at all; and, as it was only in this sense or lack of sense that the term was relevant to a plaintiff's case in libel, a corporation might well be guilty of it. He added that, even had " malice in fact " been in issue, he would, for his part, readily have imputed it.

In 1886 in *Abrath* v. *North Eastern Railway Company*[21] the scruple that had disturbed Baron Alderson excited Lord Bramwell to agony. In an action of malicious prosecution the jury found for the defendants on the ground that no malice had been proved, and the finding

---

[19] (1854) 10 Ex. 352.
[20] *Whitfield* v. *South Eastern Ry.* (1858) E.B. & E. 115.
[21] (1886) 11 App.Cas. 247.

was upheld both in the Court of Appeal and in the House of Lords. But Lord Bramwell exploded into dicta. " I am of opinion that no action for a malicious prosecution will lie against a corporation. I take this opportunity of saying that as directly and peremptorily as I possibly can; and I think the reasoning is demonstrative. To maintain [the action] it must be shown that there was . . . malice or some indirect and illegitimate motive in the prosecution. A corporation is incapable of malice or motive." It would have made no difference had the directors maliciously ordered the prosecution and had set the company's seal to their order. They were themselves but agents and would have had no authority to bind the company; and it was against them as individuals that the action should have been brought. He ended a spirited judgment on a defiant note. " It is said that this is an old-fashioned notion. It is: but this opinion is one that I have entertained ever since I have known anything about the law, and, although it is an old-fashioned one, I trust it is one which will not die out." So emotional a reaction from so prosaic a judge is at first sight surprising. Bramwell, of all men, might have been expected to cherish Dr. Johnson's advice to clear the mind of cant. But he was bred upon Adam Smith and Ricardo, and he was resolved to the last to keep the faith of a Liberal pure and undefiled. To him the yearnings of collectivism—paternal, intrusive, enervating —were anathema. It was the man that mattered; and he wished to tear aside the corporate curtain and expose the figures that lurked behind it to public view and legal sanction. A prosperous and reliant society rested upon individual enterprise and individual responsibility.[22]

Lord Bramwell's outburst was the last desperate attempt to withstand or deflect the floods of vicarious liability as they swept upon corporate bodies. When in 1899 counsel ventured to cite his dictum in yet another case of malicious prosecution, Mr. Justice Darling declined to receive it.[23] But, if he thus voiced professional opinion, he must be admitted only to have deviated into sense. He confused the distinction between " malice in law " and " malice in fact " upon which Lord Campbell had insisted, and the last sentences of his judgment revealed a mind in chaos. He should, he said, " entirely agree " with Lord Bramwell " if malice in law were synonymous with *malice* in French —a sort of *esprit* tinged with ill nature. In such a sense a corporation would be as incapable of malice as of wit. But of malice—actual malice—in a legal sense I think a corporation is capable." The words seem to defy interpretation; but comment was fortunately made superfluous by Lord Lindley's judgment in *Citizens Life Assurance Co.* v. *Brown*.[24] He set the problem in its due perspective. " If it is once granted that corporations are for civil purposes to be regarded as persons, *i.e.* as principals acting by agents or servants, it is difficult to see why the ordinary doctrines of agency

---

[22] Two years later, in an address to the British Association, Lord Bramwell indignantly denied the charges currently levied against the teaching of his masters. *Laissez-faire* harsh and Political Economy a dismal science ? " As well say that Euclid's elements are inhuman." (*A Memoir of Lord Bramwell*, 84–85.)

[23] *Cornford* v. *Carlton Bank, Ltd.* [1899] 1 Q.B. 392.

[24] [1904] A.C. 423.

and of master and servant are not to be applied to corporations as well as to ordinary individuals. . . . To talk about imputing malice to corporations appears to introduce metaphysical subtleties which are needless and fallacious."

The judges had thus succeeded, without undue effort, in fitting the new and troublesome corporation into the framework of the common law. They had afforded reasonable protection both to the public and to the shareholders who had risked their money to supply the sinews of that vast commercial and industrial enterprise which made Victoria's England the most powerful country in the world. Nor, save in the fleeting temptations of the one-man company and the ambiguities of malice, had they needed to rely upon adventitious or exotic arts. It had sufficed to scan the language of the relevant statute, a task if unpleasing at least not unfamiliar, and to apply the domestic rules of vicarious liability as if they had been concerned with human masters. They had not felt bound to reflect upon the nature of corporate personality any more than they had stooped to uncover the roots of tort. It is time to ask if the writers were more ambitious.

In 1850 was published Grant's *Practical Treatise on the Law of Corporations* and in 1875 Brice on the *Doctrine of Ultra Vires*.[25] The student of English professional literature before the last quarter of the nineteenth century will find in these books, as he will have anticipated, a large and incoherent collation of authorities. But even the most pedestrian author

[25] In 1871 Holmes had published a pioneer essay on *Ultra Vires*: see 5 Am. Law Rev., Jan. 1871.

usually deems it decent to preface the most severely practical work with some slight concession to theory; and these two writers do not, alas, disappoint expectations. Grant, in his first few pages, refers to the corporation as an " abstract being," " a metaphysical body," an *ens rationis*, " a beautiful combination of the legal characteristics of the finite being with the essentials of infinity." Brice, if less ecstatic, is no less mysterious. It is " a fiction, a shade, a nonentity, but a reality for legal purposes." It need hardly be said that, after these effusions, the authors get down to business and bother their heads no more about concept and analysis. The shade of Brice may be left in peace; but Grant, by his very eccentricity, deserves a further word. Like Willes and Manning, he was a rare medievalist among early Victorian lawyers. A devotee of black-letter editions, he lamented that he could not persuade the judges to listen with becoming deference to his citations from the Year Books.[26] Lovingly appreciated and tenderly applied, they might bridge the gap, otherwise impassable, between the medieval commune and the limited liability company. But if a stiff-necked generation would not learn from the past, it should find it hard to profit from the present; and he refused " on principle," to compile an index to the cases scattered over seven hundred pages of text.

From such writers as these, as indeed from all whose primary object is to expound the content of the law, it is unfair to expect serious investigation into the nature of personality. A more likely source is the

26 See *Keene* v. *Beard* (1860) 8 C.B. (N.S.) 372.

German jurisprudence, the weight of which fell upon English academic thought throughout the nineteenth century. The charm was felt, among others, by Lindley.[27] In the General Part of Thibaut's *System des Pandekten Rechts*, which he translated in 1855, he was introduced to the corporation, defined, at least in Lindley's rendering, as a " moral " or " ideal " person. But, though still young and not yet purged of university enthusiasms, he was already too shrewd or perhaps too insular to compromise himself in such shady company. In his notes he preferred to describe a corporation as " a judicial person distinct from its individual members " or as " a fictitious person created for a particular purpose." It was difficult, he added, " to maintain upon principle " that it could not commit a tort or even a crime. When he became a judge, while he never regretted that he had once been a jurist, he knew better than to darken decision with speculation. If he faltered at the sight of the one-man company, he refuted, with cold propriety, Lord Bramwell's extravagant approach to malice.

If Thibaut could allure, Savigny dominated. To him must be ascribed the doubtful honour of the Fiction Theory, which he associated, not without difficulty, with Roman jurisprudence and which was involved in his meditations upon the nature and function of law. " All law exists for the sake of the moral freedom indwelling in every man. The original idea of a person, as the subject of a right, must therefore coincide with the idea of man, and the identity of both ideas may be

[27] *Supra*, p. 18. See also his adventures in the field of Possession, *infra*, p. 87.

expressed in this formula: every individual man,
and only the individual man, is judicially capable."
If this premise were accepted, it followed that, when
society required the introduction into the human
compound of associations and institutions, these, while
they must be called persons, were manifestly fictions
—*dramatis personae*, allowed, for their author's convenience, to pass across the stage of law. By the same
logic they were invented, and could be destroyed, at
the will of the state. As Maitland said in 1900,[28]
the Fiction Theory led to the Concession Theory.

It is perhaps surprising that Austin, so ardent a
disciple of Savigny, should not have followed him
into this inviting field of speculation. But the course
he pursued in his lectures did not require him to
examine, or spared him the pain of examining, the
nature of a corporation. He was content with a desultory
reference to " persons so-called by a figment and for
the sake of brevity in discourse." [29] The first English
jurist to admit his debt to Savigny was Markby. In
his *Elements of Law* [30] he swallowed him whole.
" Besides human beings we find that certain abstractions
or entities, or whatever you may choose to call them,
are spoken of as holding rights and being liable to
debts and obligations." He offered an incongruous
catalogue: the City of London, a bank, a railway
company, the Government of India, an idol. All
these, he said, " are frequently spoken of as holding
property, as bringing and defending suits, as making

[28] Introduction to Gierke, *Political Theories of the Middle Age*,
XXX.
[29] Lecture XII, 354.
[30] 1st ed. (1871), 58–60.

contracts and so forth, as if they were ordinary men.
This is, of course, a pure fiction. . . . There is a
fictitious or, as I prefer to call it, a juristical person
(to distinguish it from a real person) to which all the
rights are supposed to belong and upon which all the
duties and obligations are imposed." Upon Pollock,
as upon Markby, the master had laid his
spell. But when in 1876 he published his *Principles
of Contract*, while he avowed his general admiration,
he reserved judgment on this particular issue. He was
not yet prepared to dissent from the fiction theory, but
he wore his rue with a difference. " We may call the
artificial person a fictitious substratum or substance
conceived as supporting legal attributes, remembering
always that we must think of legal fictions as derived
from *fingere* not in the modern sense of feigning but
in the sense of creating or fashioning. Nor would it
be very difficult to show, were it not a matter of metaphysical rather than legal interest, that what we call
the artificial identity of a corporation is, within its own
sphere and for its own purposes, just as real as any
other identity." [31]

Among the writers on English law who emerged
in the second half of Victoria's reign Maitland, by
general consent, stands supreme; and upon him the
light of German learning cast its most dazzling rays.
Savigny was his early hero and always retained his
affection. But he devoured voraciously the work of
the later jurists and he became aware that Savigny's
views were criticised by such scholars as Beseler and
Gierke. The old master's treatment of corporate

[31] *Principles of Contract*, 1st ed. 81.

personality fell a victim to the new research; and in 1895, when Maitland published the *History of English Law*, he turned aside from the medieval theme to announce the deposition of the fiction theory and to warn his readers that if they clung with mistaken loyalty to an outmoded faith they would fall out of step with their more learned cousins in Germany. He was prepared to show " that the theory which speaks of the corporation's personality as fictitious, a theory which English lawyers borrowed from medieval canonists, has never suited our English law very well. It should at all events be known that on the continent of Europe this doctrine no longer enjoys an undisputed orthodoxy either among the students of the Roman *universitas* or among the students of medieval and modern corporations." [32]

The passage is curious, and, in such a context and from such an author, a double curiosity. The fiction theory had been admitted by Austin without comment, and Markby had embraced it *con amore*. But Lindley, while in deference to superior erudition he had allowed it to adorn a tale, would not use it to point a moral. If here and there a modern judge paid lip-service to it, this was no more than a convention that afforded the sensation without the necessity of thought and which he never dreamed could influence his mind. Nor, despite the fragments from the Year Books collected and displayed by Maitland, is there any evidence that it excited or distressed his medieval predecessors. Pollock, it has been seen, was nervous of it and already in 1876 had prepared a way of retreat. His name

[32] Pollock and Maitland, *History of English Law*, I, 489–491.

certainly appeared on the title-page of the *History of English Law* and he must presumably have accepted joint if not several responsibility for the sentiments expressed in its pages.[33] But, five years after Maitland's death, he took the cruel occasion of a *Festschrift* offered to Gierke on his seventieth birthday to expose the error of imagining that the common law had ever received the theory.[34] From Bracton to Blackstone no writer had rested upon this or indeed upon any other hypothesis. Those Year Books already available to gentlemanly inspection offered no positive rule or coherent doctrine; and Pollock could feel comfortably assured that few students would be officious to disturb the dust that lay upon the forbidding manuscripts in college libraries or amid the Public Records. " As to saying with any certainty what language may or may not be found somewhere in the Year Books, that is impossible to any ordinary human faculties and will remain so until such time as the whole of them are critically edited and adequately indexed."

The refutation was complete and need not be repeated. Maitland had fallen a brilliant victim to his own intensive culture. As a jurist, he could not but believe that, beneath the surface of phrase and process, veiled by the homely language which reflected an instinctive reaction to immediate problems, there lay a wealth of principle waiting to be uncovered by

[33] In 1895 Pollock wrote to Holmes: " I want to tell you how little of the *History of English Law* is my writing; *viz.*, the introduction (not quite all), the chapter on Anglo-Saxon law and the bulk, not the whole, of the chapter on Early History of Contract." *Pollock–Holmes Letters*, I, 60–61.

[34] Pollock, *Essays in the Law*, 151.

devoted research. It had only to be revealed to persuade the judges that it was precisely what they had striven, half consciously, to formulate and apply. As a historian, he felt the lure of continuity. *Nouveau riche* as the commercial corporation appeared, pious hands could provide a pedigree. The vision was romantic; and Maitland might have learnt from the master of romance. Sir Walter Scott had observed that " in life many things befall every mortal of which the individual never knows the real cause or origin." [35] " Were we," he added, " to point the most marked distinction between a real and a fictitious narrative, we would say that the former, in reference to the remote causes of the events it relates, is obscure, doubtful and mysterious, whereas in the latter case it is part of the author's duty to afford satisfactory details upon the causes of the events he has recorded. In a word, he must account for everything." The scholar, like any other artist, seeks to satisfy his aesthetic conscience by " composing " his material and " placing " it in its proper setting. He likes to tie the loose ends of his tale. But the design is perilous. To be tidy is a temptation that he must steel himself to resist.

The Fiction Theory, if never acclimatised in England, had certainly flourished in Germany. But even there it had become unfashionable; and Maitland, when he noted its passing, marked also its successor. In its place, he wrote, " we are to see a living organism and a real person, with body and members and a will of its own, . . . a group-person with a group-will." " This theory," he admitted, " which we might call

[35] Introduction to *The Abbot*.

Realism, may seem to carry its head among the clouds. But a serious attempt has been made to give it feet that walk upon the earth." [36]   Pollock, sceptical as he had been of its forerunner, was prepared to welcome the new revelation. In the seventh edition of his *Principles of Contract*, published in 1902, he described the Realist Theory as " not only more philosophical but more business-like." It is difficult to share this enthusiasm. " Realism " itself, save in the jargon of the philosopher, is an empty word. It was not born with meaning and cannot be said to have achieved it: it must have meaning thrust upon it. In the present context the effort seems neither successful nor rewarding. To dissect the limited liability company in terms of the human body demands a desperate stretch of the imagination, and a simple lawyer may be excused for thinking that the " real " theory is even more unrealistic than the " fiction."

The waters are deep. English judges have been careful not to dip in them; and it is significant that Holmes here preferred the empiricism of the Bench to the mirage of scholarship. When he returned thanks for the *Festschrift* to Gierke which Pollock had sent him in 1911, he wrote that he had " never realised the Corporation entity question as a very burning one," and he had earlier confessed his failure " to find in these discourses about corporations, partnerships and charitable foundations, much except mares' nests." [37] Holmes' indifference, whether it was intuitive or calculated, is readily forgiven, at least on this side of the

[36] Introduction to Gierke, *Political Theories of the Middle Age*, xxvi.
[37] *Pollock–Holmes Letters*, I, 115, 174.

Atlantic. Cardinal Newman declared that " it is not at all easy to wind up an Englishman to a dogmatic level." [38] To this especial charge of intellectual apathy the lawyer as well as the layman may cheerfully plead guilty.

---

[38] *Apologia*, 190. It is perhaps permissible to include New England in the scope of this generalisation.

CHAPTER 4

POSSESSION

THE language of their art, inherited by the Victorian lawyers, contained no word more familiar than Possession. It had for generations been the hallmark of Trespass: in Trover it played a more difficult and ambiguous role: it was the central feature of Larceny, and the narrow interpretation there placed upon it left gaps that were belatedly filled by piecemeal legislation. But, if familiar, no word in his lexicon, unless it be Causation, was calculated to strike the ear of an English lawyer with a more horrid sound. Whether from apprehension or lethargy, no definition had been attempted before the nineteenth century. The profession had been content to accept it as a cardinal element of civil and criminal liability and to decide whether, as a matter of casuistry, it might be said to exist in any given set of facts.

Once again it was the pre-eminence of the German jurists that stimulated curiosity, and once again Austin, through whose devotion their message might have been expected to reach English ears, disappoints the reader. His examination of Possession was prevented by the collapse of his health and the ruin of his hopes. When in 1826 the foundation of the University of London encouraged the prospect of academic legal study, he was appointed the Professor of Jurisprudence; and his first lecture was bright with promise. " The

class," his widow wrote,[1] " exceeded his expectations."
He was " impressed and excited by the spectacle of a
noble band of young men, and he felt with a sort of
awe the responsibility attaching to his office." Youth,
however generous, is rarely single-minded, and few
were noble enough to endure to the end. The seasoned
lecturer is inured to the progressive erosion of his
audience; but Austin was innocent and sensitive.
His vocation was to teach, and if he failed in this he
must despair. " I was born out of time and place,"
he said. " I ought to have been a schoolman of the
twelfth century—or a German professor." So, on
June 29, 1832, he gave his last lecture, his course
unfinished; and it was on this day that he had proposed
to discuss the nature of Possession. Only fragmentary
notes remain to cheat the hope he had cherished of
examining " the anomalous and perplexed right of
possession " and towards which he had intended " to
borrow from a celebrated treatise by Von Savigny
entitled *Das Recht des Besitzes* or *De Jure Possessionis*;
of all books which I pretend to know accurately the
least alloyed with error and imperfection." [2]

It would be irrelevant and presumptuous to attempt
here any serious scrutiny of the book to which Austin
paid so full a tribute, especially as Savigny's thesis,
whatever its merits as a reconstruction of the Roman
texts, has at least the virtue of apparent simplicity. It
is enough to say that for him Possession had always a
physical and a mental element. A person must stand

[1] See the Preface by Sarah Austin to the 1861 edition of her
husband's works.
[2] *Outline of the Course of Lectures*, 5th ed., 53.

in a physical relation to an object (*corpus*) and he must intend to deal with it as his own (*animus domini*). If he exercised control with this purpose in his mind, then and then only might he properly be said to possess. From those rare English lawyers who were tempted to reflect upon the nature of the concepts they used, an exposition so lucid and so highly recommended met with an immediate response. Nor was it to be restricted to the needs of a single system, Roman or German: it must have a general, perhaps a universal, significance.

It is not surprising that, for the first half of Victoria's reign, such thought as was spared in England upon the nature of Possession was dominated by Savigny. In 1848 his book was translated by Sir Erskine Perry. Perry was Chief Justice of the Supreme Court of Bombay and he dedicated the translation to the " members of the Honourable Company's service engaged in the administration of justice in India." [3] He acclaimed Savigny's book as " the most celebrated treatise of modern times " and he offered the testimonial of Dr. Arnold that its author was " the greatest master of Roman Law in Europe." It was peculiarly suitable for the servants of the East India Company who were to fulfil their mission unencumbered by the tedious and irrational technicalities of the common law, but it might also illumine, if it could not sweeten, the dark and dusty corners of Westminster Hall.

In 1855, when Lindley translated Thibaut, he added

---

[3] Four years later, when he retired, Perry occupied himself, with strange ingratitude, in advocating the abolition of the Honourable Company.

an appendix on Possession. Upon this subject, he lamented, there was not in England " any work, good, bad or indifferent." Blackstone was most unsatisfactory. " Not only had he attributed no definite meaning to the word *possession*, but he had constantly confused ideas so very distinct as the right *to* possess and the right *of* possession." If, indeed, any native doctrine existed, it was " only to be found by wading through a mass of cases upon the old possessory actions, ejectment, trespass, trover and larceny." From this confusion it was refreshing to turn to the orderly German mind. Thibaut was not, perhaps, on this occasion at his happiest; but his deficiencies were more than supplied by Savigny. *His* essay was " universally recognised as one of the most masterly that had ever appeared upon any branch of Jurisprudence," and Lindley commended it to the " careful perusal of the English student," whose illiteracy, he noted, had been pampered by Perry's translation.

Savigny's progress had so far been triumphant. Sir Henry Maine in his *Ancient Law* was the first to strike a jarring note. " Few educated persons are so little versed in legal literature as not to have heard that the language of the Roman jurisconsults on the subject of Possession long occasioned the greatest possible perplexity and that the genius of Savigny is supposed to have chiefly proved itself by the solution which he discovered for the enigma." [4] This sly glance was directed not so much upon the jurist as on the Romanist;

---

[4] Chap. VIII: " The early history of Property."

and Markby, in the *Elements of Law*, noted the reservation and took the distinction.[5]   Just as he had welcomed Savigny's Fiction Theory, so now he borrowed his doctrine of Possession. If it had to be stripped of its Roman accretions, this served only to emphasise its cosmopolitan validity. The core of the doctrine was the coincidence of a physical and a mental element, and these might well take different shapes in different times and places. The *animus domini*, indeed, scarcely suited the English climate. In England the bailee was the typical possessor precisely because he did not purport to act as owner. But to substitute another *animus* was not to impair the doctrine, and Markby was ready with his own variant: "the determination to exercise physical power on one's own behalf."

In the second half of Victoria's reign Savigny's position was more openly and more fatally challenged. In Germany his interpretation of the Roman texts was rejected, and, as Gierke had shattered his theory of Corporate Personality, so Ihering took his place as the fashionable exponent of Possession. As is the wont of academic controversy, Ihering was perhaps more powerful to destroy than to construct; but this was not likely to lessen his appeal to the few English students whose ears were attuned to hear him. They had been proud to follow Savigny. But in thought as in dress times change, and it did not do to be dowdy. In two essays entitled *Possession in the Roman Law* Lightwood in 1887 and Bond in 1890 announced Savigny's deposition[6]; but, while they acclaimed the new prophet,

[5] See sections 314–334.
[6] 3 L.Q.R. 32; 6 L.Q.R. 259.

they still looked wistfully for some comprehensive principle that would embrace not only the glories of Rome and Germany but even the modest needs of their own island. Now that the stumbling-block of *animus domini* had been removed, the common law might surely claim kinship with the Corpus Juris Civilis. Lightwood was both bold and ingenious. A number of non-owners had been allowed to possess in Rome. " Extend the list," he cried, " and we are in English law " [7]—a short cut, indeed, across the frontiers of national culture.

Ihering's message, however, percolated too slowly through the sluggish English minds to influence the makers of the common law, and it had now to compete with attempts to construct a doctrine of Possession out of domestic materials. Holmes took the initiative. He indignantly, nay disdainfully, rejected the claims of the Germans and the Romanists to monopolise philosophy and jurisprudence. " It will be a service to sound thinking to show that a far more civilised system than the Roman is framed upon a plan which is irreconcilable with the *a priori* doctrines of Kant and Hegel." [8] Like Markby, he stressed the key position

---

[7] 3 L.Q.R. 52–53. So, too, Bond in 6 L.Q.R. at 278–279: " Ihering has in his other works remarked on the great similarity of the Roman and English characters as seen in the development of their legal systems. It may be said without fear of contradiction that his is the only German theory of Possession in which an English lawyer would recognise the principles which underlie our own common law."

[8] *The Common Law*, Lecture VI. Holmes nevertheless knew the German jurisprudence and acclaimed Ihering as " a man of genius." Savigny, however, was " the only writer with whom English readers are generally acquainted ": see pp. 206–209, 218–219.

of bailment. Whatever the rights of his Roman equiva-
lents, the English bailee was *par excellence* the possessor.
He felt, somewhat too ingenuously, that the first call
upon a legal concept was to fit the facts; and any
common law theory of possession must therefore
accept and explain the status of the bailee. But even
Holmes still thought in terms of *animus* and *corpus*.
He was more heavily indoctrinated than he realised
with Teutonic-Romanesque language if not with its
sentiment. Necessarily rejecting Savigny's *animus domini*
he replaced it with an " intent to exclude others." Such
an intent, he believed, was " all that the common law
deems needful, and on principle no more should be
required."

Fired by the example of Holmes, Pollock set himself
to write a " systematic account " of possession in
England.[9] He found that Mr. R. S. Wright was
independently and simultaneously embarked on a
similar venture. Wright had been a distinguished
classical scholar and a favourite pupil of Jowett at
Balliol. It is recorded that, when in 1890 he became
a judge, " his simple tastes and radical opinions made
him unwilling to accept the honour of knighthood." [10]
But he thought of his colleagues, stifled his scruples and
swallowed the title. Like Blackburn and Lindley, he
was jurist as well as judge: unlike them, he was not a
success on the Bench. Too impulsive and too impatient
for a court of first instance, he died before he could
adorn the Court of Appeal. It is more pleasant to
retrieve from his later years a picture of idyllic

[9] Preface to *Possession in the Common Law*.
[10] D.N.B.

democracy. He enjoyed the recreations of a gentleman-farmer in Hertfordshire. There, " seated under a tree, he would invite the opinions of his labourers and decide upon the course to be pursued in accordance with the views of the majority." Pollock found so cultivated a mind refreshingly congenial to his project, and they combined to produce in 1888 an *Essay on Possession in the Common Law*. This, they insisted, was " a composite and not a joint effort "; but it is clear from Wright's contribution that he was satisfied to accept his companion's analysis. Pollock followed Holmes both in the claim that the common law had its own indigenous doctrine of Possession and in retaining the dichotomy of *animus* and *corpus*. But he offered his own rendering of *animus*: the intent to exercise physical control " in one's own name and against the world at large." When the two elements were fused, " we have possession in law as well as fact." It would undoubtedly be easier if legal language chimed with popular speech. But " no system of law had gone to that length." [11]

It is not uninteresting to speculate why both Holmes and Pollock persisted in the pursuit of the elusive *animus*. They had, indeed, been brought up amid its mysteries and the cult had survived the deflation of Savigny. But they were faced with a more material problem—the troublesome case of the servant. To him, at least in certain circumstances and for certain purposes, the common law denied possession; and it was for this reason that Pollock insisted that control must be exercised " in one's own name." A word

[11] *Possession in the Common Law*, 16–17.

must therefore be spared upon the place of the servant both in civil and in criminal liability. In tort it was clear that, where a master had left his house or his goods in the charge of a servant, it was the master and not the servant who could bring Trespass against a third party.[12] In the criminal law the distinction between larceny and embezzlement was a commonplace of nineteenth-century practitioners. The master who put his goods into the hands of his servant retained possession, and the servant, if he misappropriated them, committed larceny. But if a third party handed goods to the servant to take to his master, the servant at once obtained possession and could not be guilty of larceny. It was to fill this gap that the crime of embezzlement had been invented or applied by a statute of 1800.[13]

Holmes was worried by these eccentricities. To meet them he returned to the supposed survival in the common law of fragments or recollections of slavery to which he had been driven in an attempt to palliate the doctrine of vicarious liability.[14] If the English servant were the descendant, however illegitimate, of the Roman *servus*, this would explain both his impotence in trespass and his capacity for larceny. The hypothesis was not only extravagant: it did not meet the facts. It would indeed be strange if the slave or his progeny, who necessarily lacked personality to possess goods entrusted to him by his owner, should suddenly achieve

---

[12] *Bertie* v. *Beaumont* (1812) 16 East 33; *Mayhew* v. *Suttle* (1854) 4 E. & B. 347; *White* v. *Bailey* (1861) 10 C.B.(N.S.) 227.

[13] *R.* v. *Bazeley* (1799) 2 Leach 825; *R.* v. *Reed* (1854) Dearsley 168, 257.

[14] *Supra,* p. 52. Holmes, *The Common Law,* 226–229.

it when given them by a third party. It seems clear, moreover, that as late as the seventeenth century it was only so long as the servant remained in the master's house that he was denied possession. Once he passed into the street the possession passed with him.[15] Antiquarian reconstruction, however resolute, was therefore irrelevant. Pollock, when with Maitland he exposed the fallacy, was careful not to fall into the opposite error of *ex post facto* rationalisation. If there were anomalies, they had better be noted and endured. Nor was the law so far removed as it might seem from popular opinion. " In a great number of cases the servant may be said not even to have possession in fact, for he would not be supposed by any ordinary observer to have the physical custody of the thing otherwise than on his master's behalf and at his master's disposal." [16]

This discussion of the servant's idiosyncrasies, if it is a digression, is nevertheless significant. It suggests that the common lawyers have normally thought of Possession in terms of physical control and that, save for those still influenced, consciously or through vain repetition, by Roman or German analogies, it is not necessary, or desirable, to search for any *animus*, bold or faint, plausible or laborious. It may be admitted that no person will be granted the legal advantages of possession unless he is exercising a conscious control either of a particular object or at least of the area in

---

[15] See Y.B. 18 and 19 Edw. III (R.S.) 508; Y.B. 21 Hen. VII, Hil. pl. 21; Coke, *Third Institute*, c. 47; Hale, *Pleas of the Crown*, 506.

[16] *Possession in the Common Law*, 58–59; Pollock and Maitland, *Hist. of Eng. Law*, II, 528.

which that object happens to be. But if this relation must be assumed to comprise a mental element, the *animus* involved is itself neither more nor less than an aspect of *corpus*—one of the factors upon which the claim to control rests. The validity of this analysis may be tested by turning from the jurists to the judges and by observing their reaction to one question which is central to the whole problem of Possession. Must a person who claims to possess an object know of its existence ? The question may be put in another form. Does control of a given area carry with it control, and therefore possession, of everything within that area ? The cases in which the point has arisen have been scrutinised with an intensity which it would be hazardous to emulate and impertinent to repeat.[17] But it may yet be worth while to see how far they were argued on principle and whether, even if inadvertently or by implication, the judges have left clues to the nature of the possession whose presence or absence they had to determine.

In the nineteenth century law of Torts a trilogy of cases has become in retrospect, if not famous, at least notorious. In *Bridges* v. *Hawkesworth* in 1851 [18] the crucial issue was whether a shopkeeper possessed a parcel of bank notes lying on the floor of his shop which had been dropped by some person unknown and of the very existence of which he was ignorant.

---

[17] Goodhart, *Essays in Common Law and Jurisprudence*, Chap. 4; Carter, " Taking and the Acquisition of Possession in Larceny," 14 M.L.R. 27; Turner, *Modern Approach to Criminal Law*, 356.
[18] (1851) 21 L.J.Q.B. 75; 15 Jurist 1079.

Counsel ranged far and wide in their search for per-
suasive authority: Puffendorff, Blackstone, the Digest,
even the Book of Deuteronomy were pressed into
service. But the happy chance of Perry's recent translation made Savigny the most attractive focus of
argument, and a spirited discussion revolved around
his text and meaning. Mr. Justice Patteson, however,
while he joined in the discussion, was careful, when he
gave judgment, not to allow his learning to lead him
too far from the facts. He paid Savigny a graceful
compliment and dismissed him. As Dr. Goodhart
has pointed out, it is not easy to discover the *ratio
decidendi* of the case. One pregnant sentence may be
quoted. " The notes never were in the custody of the
defendant nor within the protection of his house before
they were found." He did not possess because he
did not control.

In 1886 in *Elwes* v. *Brigg Gas Co.*[19] the court had
to decide if a tenant for life had possession of a prehistoric boat that lay hidden six feet beneath the surface
of the soil. Savigny was now relegated to the study
and replaced by the more familiar language of Holmes
on the Common Law. Mr. Justice Chitty held that the
tenant possessed the boat because he controlled the
land. " The boat was embedded in the land. A mere
trespasser could not have taken possession of it; he
could only have come at it by further acts of trespass
involving spoil and waste of the inheritance." [20] A

---

[19] (1886) 33 Ch.D. 562.
[20] *Ibid.*, at p. 568. Of Mr. Justice (later Lord Justice) Chitty,
Pollock wrote: " He can hardly be reckoned among the great
English judges, but he was one of the most efficient." He was,
however, " the best amateur wicket-keeper in England and

similar question was posed ten years later in *South Staffordshire Water Co.* v. *Sharman*.[21] Did a freeholder possess two rings that lay, unknown to him, at the bottom of a pool on his land ? The book now cited was Pollock and Wright on *Possession*; and Lord Russell ventured, with its support, to summarise the law. " The general principle seems to me to be that, where a person has possession of house or land with a manifest intention to exercise control over it and the things which may be upon or in it, then, if something is found on that land, whether by an employee of the owner [22] or by a stranger, the presumption is that the possession of that thing is in the owner [22] of the *locus in quo*."

Around this trilogy controversy has long raged and reconciliation is difficult. But it would seem that, for the purposes of the English law of Torts, ignorance that a particular thing exists is not a fatal bar to possession. The judges were not thinking in terms of *animus* save, if at all, as an element of *corpus*. The question throughout was whether the thing claimed was within the range of the claimant's control. If, as is often urged, *Bridges* v. *Hawkesworth* was wrongly decided, the error was one of fact not of law. Were the notes, or were they not, within the area of control exercised by the shopkeeper ? All three cases, whatever their authority, are remarkable for the attention paid

the finest oar on the river." He had indeed been an Oxford rowing Blue, and this at least suggested him as the appropriate judge to decide the fate of a prehistoric boat. See Pollock, *For my Grandson*, 174–175.

[21] [1896] 2 Q.B. 44.

[22] For " owner " in the text of the report should be read " possessor."

by judge and counsel to the jurists.   Mr. Justice Patteson, it is true, felt that he had done all that politeness required in saluting Savigny with a nod of friendly recognition. But the opinions of Holmes and Pollock were canvassed with a lively sense of their importance and in revealing contrast with the indifference shown to theories of corporate personality. Nor was this interest purely ephemeral. In April 1900 two ships, the *Winkfield* and the *Mexican*, collided in a fog off Table Bay. The *Winkfield* was at fault and the *Mexican* sank. The Postmaster-General sued for the value of the mail that the *Mexican* had been carrying, and the claim was resisted on the ground that, as the Postmaster-General was admittedly not answerable to the owners of the lost mail, he could not recover damages from a third party.[23] The case posed the riddle propounded by Holmes in his lectures. Was a bailee normally entitled to sue because he was liable to the bailor, or was he liable to the bailor because he was the only person who could sue?[24]   If English law preferred the first alternative, the present plaintiff must fail: if the second, he would win. The Court of Appeal answered the riddle in the Postmaster-General's favour. As bailee he was the classic possessor of the common law. His right of action was derived from this position and could not be affected by the relation in which he stood to his own bailor. The problem had a peculiarly academic flavour, but even the most hardened practitioners felt its attraction. Renewing their youth, they plunged into speculation. The Attorney-General, afterwards Lord

---

[23] *The Winkfield* [1902] P. 42.
[24] Holmes, *The Common Law*, 167, 170.

Finlay, cited not only Holmes but Bracton. Mr. Pickford, afterwards Lord Sterndale, replied with Pollock and Maitland and the Year Books. Mr. Scrutton, silent, but austere, watched the case for the owners of the *Mexican.* The Master of the Rolls in his judgment was no less learned. He reviewed an extensive range of literature from Kent to Holmes in America and from Coke to Maitland in England.

The effect of knowledge on possession has had to be debated in the sphere of criminal no less than in that of civil liability. There is no inherent reason, save for an idealist in search of the absolute, why possession in each branch of the law should bear the same meaning. It is true that, when Pollock and Wright in their book displayed the tortious and criminal aspects of their subject in separate parts, this arrangement was fortuitous. They did not start from the premise that distinct treatment was demanded; and Wright entitled his own contribution " Possession and Trespass in relation to the law of Theft." But hints of segregation may be culled from the reports. As early as 1743 a judge had observed " a great difference " between the possession sufficient to support a civil action and that required to sustain a prosecution, and in 1854 Lord Campbell seems to have accepted and applied the distinction.[25] In the criminal law, moreover, the analysis of possession has been complicated by the need to determine the meaning of " taking ": a word, relevant indeed to trespass as well as to larceny, but in the latter context

[25] *R.* v. *Waite* (1743) 2 East P.C. 571; *R.* v. *Reed* (1854) Dearsley 168, 257.

invested by protracted and inconclusive arguments with a sinister ambiguity.[26]

It is useful to begin with the case of *Merry* v. *Green*.[27] The plaintiff had bought the defendant's bureau at an auction. There was conflicting evidence as to whether the auctioneer had sold the bureau with or without its contents, and the point had not been left to the jury, Unknown to all concerned, there was a secret drawer in which lay a purse with money. When the bureau was delivered to the plaintiff, he discovered the hidden treasure and kept it. The defendant demanded it and, on the plaintiff's refusal, arrested him on a charge of theft. The plaintiff sued the defendant for assault and false imprisonment. The vital question was whether the plaintiff had been guilty of larceny: only thus could the arrest be justified.

Baron Parke gave the judgment of the court. He started with the assumption, which a layman might be forgiven for accepting as obvious, that a person who possessed a desk possessed also its contents, even if he could not offer a *catalogue raisonnée* of the individual items. So long, therefore, as the seller possessed the bureau he possessed the purse, ignorant though he was of its existence; and when the bureau passed into the possession of the buyer, the possession of the purse inevitably passed with it. But was the buyer's possession lawful or unlawful ? While the seller had agreed to transfer the bureau, it was doubtful if he had agreed to transfer the purse, and a new trial was ordered to

[26] See Carter, "Taking and the Acquisition of Possession in Larceny," 14 M.L.R. 27.
[27] (1841) 7 M. & W. 623.

decide this point. If at the sale the auctioneer had included the contents, there had been a "delivery" of the purse and no larceny had been committed. If the contents had been excluded from the sale, the purse had not been "delivered" but "taken". The buyer would then have begun with a trespass and his subsequent *animus furandi* would have converted it into a larceny. Baron Parke was not concerned to analyse jural concepts. But within its limits his exposition was masterly. It rested upon two propositions: that knowledge of a particular object was not necessary to possession, and that the distinction between a "delivery" and a "taking" was vital both in tort and in crime.

In 1853 a strong court met to consider the case of *R. v. Riley.*[28] On a misty October morning the prisoner drove his twenty-nine lambs out of a field. With them he inadvertently included a lamb owned by the prosecutor. Four days later he offered the flock for sale; and, when a prospective purchaser observed that it comprised thirty lambs, the prisoner, though he must now have realised the truth, sold the prosecutor's lamb with the rest. He was charged with larceny at the Durham Quarter Sessions. The Chairman thought that, for the prisoner to be convicted, he must have determined to treat the prosecutor's lamb as his own at the very instant of "taking" it, and he directed the jury that he "took" it when, and only when, he knew that it was in his flock. The jury found that he did not know this fact when he drove the lambs out of the field, but that he was guilty of felony when it was pointed out to him. After conviction the case was

[28] (1853) Dearsley 149.

remitted for consideration to the Court for Crown
Cases Reserved.

In the course of the argument Chief Baron Pollock [29]
saw the propriety of separating the passing of possession
and the " taking " of the lamb; and he alarmed counsel
by asking him to define possession. But, like Pilate,
he would not stay for an answer, and, when he came
to deliver judgment, the moment of illumination had
passed. He now treated the two processes as identical
and upheld the conviction on the ground that, as the
prisoner was a trespasser from the beginning, the
subsequent *animus furandi* made him a thief. Baron
Parke in substance repeated his reasoning in *Merry* v.
Green. The possession of the lamb passed to the
prisoner when he drove it out of the field. This act
was done without the prosecutor's consent and was
therefore not a delivery but a taking. He then added a
refinement. The trespass continued step by step until
the fatal act of appropriation converted it into a larceny;
once a trespasser, always a trespasser and at length a
felon. His judgment was typically learned and force-
ful. But it is a pity that he was not moved to ask if
" taking " bore the same meaning in trespass and in
larceny. The initial act of driving the lamb from the
field might be translated in three different ways into
legal language. Possession, it might be said, passed at
that instant to the prisoner or it remained with the

---

[29] The Lord Chief Baron was tough but not subtle. The son of
a saddler, he was born in 1783, became Chief Baron of the
Exchequer in 1844, resigned in 1866 and died in 1870. He
was twice married and had twenty-four children. One of his
grandsons was Sir Frederick Pollock, the jurist, and another
Lord Hanworth, Master of the Rolls. See *Lord Chief Baron
Pollock*, a biography by Lord Hanworth.

prosecutor or it was now in nobody. To admit the second interpretation involves a defiance of common sense too drastic for the most chambered pedant. To yield to the third would carry unhappy consequences. If the lamb had no possessor, it could presumably be removed by a stranger with impunity. The law abhors a vacuum and would certainly shrink from so licentious a conclusion. The first interpretation remains. But, if it is to be adopted and the conviction sustained, it would be prudent to divorce the passing of possession from the act of taking. The prisoner possessed in ignorance: he took with knowledge.

Two cases, the one in 1859 and the other in 1873, require a brief reference. In *R.* v. *Rowe* [30] the prisoner had been found guilty of stealing 16 cwt. of iron from the Glamorgan Canal Co. The canal had been drained in order to be cleaned and in the process the iron lay exposed upon its bed. In sustaining the conviction Chief Baron Pollock wasted no words. The iron, he thought, while it lay still unknown on the bed of the canal, might be equated to goods left behind in an inn by a guest. The landlord, and therefore the canal company, had " sufficient possession to maintain an indictment for larceny." The analogy may be suspected; but it is at least clear that the Chief Baron dismissed knowledge as irrelevant to possession. While this case has aroused little interest, that of *R.* v. *Middleton* [31] has provoked a literature that it scarcely deserves. It is, in truth, one of those tiresome cases where a miserable man, guilty of petty dishonesty,

[30] (1859) 1 Bell C.C. 93.
[31] (1873) L.R. 2 C.C.R. 38.

becomes the *corpus vile* of professional controversy.
The prisoner had been convicted at the Central Criminal
Court of stealing £8 16s. 10d. from the Postmaster-
General and had now to endure further argument in
the Court for Crown Cases Reserved. Five judges
failed to agree and were reinforced by eleven more,
In the result twelve judges, on three different grounds.
upheld the conviction and four dissented. The thirty-
six pages in which their lucubrations are recorded are
singularly barren. Lord Bramwell alone rewards the
reader. He felt that possession in the common law
bore one aspect in trespass and another in larceny and
that niceties tolerable in the former context were
despicable in the latter. " I think," he said, " that the
criminal law ought to be reasonable and intelligible.
Certainly a man who had to be hung owing to a subtle
distinction might well complain, and it is to be remembered that we must hold that to be the law now which
would have been law when such a felony was capital."
His colleagues had allowed themselves to be swayed
by a misguided view of policy. They " seem to me to
reason thus: the prisoner was as bad as a thief (which
I deny), and, being as bad, ought to be treated as one
(which I deny also)."

The academic *cheval de bataille* is the case of *R.* v.
Ashwell.[32] The facts are simple and familiar. The
prisoner asked the prosecutor to lend him a shilling.
The prosecutor handed him a coin which both believed
to be a shilling but which was in fact a sovereign. The
prisoner went away with the coin in his pocket and,
when later he realised that it was a sovereign, kept it for

[32] (1885) 16 Q.B.D. 190.

himself. With this recital simplicity ends. At the Assizes Mr. Justice Denman declined to withdraw the case from the jury: though the facts were humble, the legal issues were too rich for any tribunal save the Court for Crown Cases Reserved. The jury found a special verdict in which they described the prisoner's conduct as fraudulent and added that " if it were competent to them to find the prisoner guilty, they meant to do so." A verdict of guilty was entered and the case reserved. A formidable array of judges met, as in *R.* v. *Middleton,* to hear the arguments and another thirty-six pages were filled with confused and conflicting views. If the debate were long, the conclusion was grotesque. The court was equally divided and the conviction therefore stood—a rare if doubtful tribute to the English judicial process.

Of the seven judgments sustaining the conviction those of Mr. Justice Cave and Lord Coleridge may be examined. Mr. Justice Cave was unhappy. Misunderstanding Baron Parke in *Merry* v. *Green,* he assumed that knowledge was vital to possession. The prisoner began to possess the coin only when he knew it to be a sovereign and the *animus furandi* thus synchronised with the passing of possession. This solution makes heavy demands upon the reader's credulity. He may be forgiven if he asks when a person does possess a coin if not when it is, to his knowledge, in his pocket.[33] Lord Coleridge began with the safe statement that

[33] If, as Mr. Justice Cave seemed to think, it was a question of identifying the coin in terms of value, he was unwittingly introducing into the criminal law the distinction rejected in the English law of contract between *error in corpore* and *error in substantia.*

there could be no larceny at common law without a trespass and that, where the possession of goods has passed, it is necessary to distinguish a " delivery " from a " taking." He might then have been expected to pursue the hint dropped if not appreciated by Chief Baron Pollock in *R.* v. *Riley* and stress the special significance of " taking " in the criminal law. He did indeed conclude that the prisoner " did not take the coin till he knew what he had got; and when he knew what he had got, that same instant he stole it." This, as he himself said, was " good sense." But, though it may also have been " good law," the links in his own chain of reasoning are missing.

Of those who would have quashed the conviction Mr. Justice Stephen was the most impressive. He was incensed at his brother Cave's submission that possession did not pass and that the coin was not "taken" until the prisoner realised what it was that he had got; and he dissected the unfortunate judge's logic with merciless precision. It involved the artificial interpretation either of " possession " or of " taking " or of both words. " If the word *possession* is chosen to be interpreted, this is done by explaining it to mean something beyond actual control over the thing possessed, namely, control coupled with knowledge, which may or may not exist. If the word *taking* is chosen to be interpreted, it is assumed in this case to mean, not an actual physical taking, but a subsequent change of mind relating back to such physical taking. I know of no authority for either of these fictions. The word *possession* is indeed used in many senses, some of them highly artificial, but this is a bad reason for adding a new artificial meaning to it." The other judges who would have quashed the conviction accepted Stephen's analysis; and Mr. Justice Matthew and Mr. Justice Field expressly dissented from the assumption that, because the prisoner had been dishonest, it was their duty to find some legal excuse, however thin, for convicting him of a crime.

These cases, civil and criminal alike, offer an extraneous interest to those who indulge the insular sport of chasing the *ratio decidendi*. If it is incumbent not only to kill but to dismember the elusive quarry, the judgments are disagreeably recalcitrant. It may well be discreet to acknowledge that the judicial process is not a science, reducible to rule and formula, but an art whose practice involves as much instinct as instruction. But the earnest if ingenuous student in pursuit of a principle, when he has struggled manfully through the turgid pages in which he must fain hope it lies concealed, emerges unenlightened and unrefreshed. Though the judges suffer the idea of possession to pass and re-pass across the surface of their minds and though at times they are uneasily conscious that it deserves definition, they can hardly be said to have braced themselves to the task. Parke, Bramwell and Stephen alone leave a firm impression: the first because, if his subtlety sank too easily into technicality, his judgments display a characteristic clarity of thought and a power of relentless reasoning; the two others because of their forthright rejection of anything that savoured of pedantry.

It must be confessed that up to the close of Victoria's reign neither judge nor jurist had succeeded in constructing a doctrine that was at once coherent and realistic. Most judges denied that knowledge of a specific object was essential to its possession and ignored *animus* as an alien and unwanted intruder. Their reactions, however, differed to civil and to criminal liability. It is true that they started with the brave assertion that every larceny involved a trespass and every trespass an absence of consent. But, as the arguments proceeded, they scarcely appeared to be thinking of possession in identical terms in the two branches of their jurisdiction, or, if they were, to be directing their appreciation of it, hazy and undefined as this might be, to identical ends. It is tempting to borrow a phrase created by a later generation to salvage the Law of Nature and to speak of a " Law of Possession with a changing content." But an intellectual abstraction is not like a physical instrument that can be used for a number of diverse operations and yet remain the same. It is more candid to admit even in the common law a double prospect of possession. When a lawyer claims for a thesis the attribute of universal validity, it may cool his ardour to remember Dr. Johnson's story of the Lichfield shoemaker who published a spelling-book and dedicated it to the Universe.

The suspicion that possession is a word charged with more than one meaning, not only in different countries but within the bounds of a single legal system, is deepened when it is set against the notion of Seisin. For centuries this concept dominated the English land law and upon it pivoted the whole machinery of conveyancing. Etymologically, and perhaps technically, it was at first a synonym of possession, and it has often been identified with it. Maitland was fascinated by the

word and its implications, and, at his magic touch, a
" mystery " became a " beatitude." But, if blessed, it
did not cease at once to be mysterious. In 1885 he
said of Bracton that with him seisin was " simply
possession—a pure matter of fact." In 1888 he felt
able to write of " Bracton's theory of possession."
In 1895 he pronounced or restated the dogma that
" Seisin is possession," to be " sharply opposed to
proprietary right." [34] It has since been demonstrated
that this equation betrays a misunderstanding of the
nature and place of seisin in the medieval law. Maitland,
here as elsewhere, would not leave his native genius
to its own conclusions. He lent too heavily upon the
German masters he revered—Hensler on Bracton,
Savigny on everybody, Ihering on Savigny. The gulf,
indeed, is wide between seisin and possession, at least
as the latter word is used in tort and in crime. Seisin
was essentially a medieval concept with a *mystique* of
its own, " an enjoyment of property based upon title
and not essentially distinguishable from right." [35]
The English conveyancers recognised not a unity but
a hierarchy of seisins, each with its own complementary
action: the writ of right, the writ of entry, mort
d'ancestor, novel disseisin. As Maitland had been
misled by the Germans, so the Germans had misunderstood the Romans. Comparisons between different legal systems in different ages are as perilous as

[34] Maitland, *Collected Papers*, I; *The Seisin of Chattels*, 344–345;
The Mystery of Seisin, 378; *The Beatitude of Seisin*, 432. See
also *History of English Law*, II, 29, 33.
[35] Plucknett, *Concise Hist. of the Common Law*, 5th ed., 357–358.
See also the learned author's *Legislation of Edward I*, 53, and
his summary in *Harvard Law Review*, xl, 921 of Joüon des
Longrais, *La Conception anglaise de la saisine.*

they are alluring. But, if English is to be compared with Roman law, seisin is much nearer to Roman *possessio* than the latter is to English possession. " Roman *possessio*," Professor Lawson has said, " is, in principle, the practical and economic aspect of ownership." [36] This sentence not ineptly describes common law seisin: it is far removed from the possession of trespass and of larceny.

The last word may be spoken by Pollock, not pontifically as the jurist but in his leisure moments and stripped of illusion. Writing to Holmes on the dangers of definition, he stressed the existence of two different problems. " You may want to analyse the past and present uses of a term (let X = Right or Possession or anything), to find out what idea, if any, is really common to all the significations and whether you can make a pedigree of them . . . Or you may want to decide whether any and what conventional limitation of the term will be useful for the particular job you are on." " Plain enough," he added, " but many writers muddle it." [37] It would be unkind to ask if Pollock himself always avoided confusion. But the story of Possession in the reign of Victoria serves at least to underline his warning. The jurists busied themselves with the first of his problems and lost their way, pursuing the myth of universality. The judges concentrated upon the second, but with so narrow a vision that, even for their " particular job " in tort or crime, any lessons they left to their successors have proved of doubtful value.

[36] *Roman Law and Common Law*, 2nd ed., 72–74.
[37] *Pollock–Holmes Letters*, I, 228.

CHAPTER 5

CRIMINAL LIABILITY

THE current books on the criminal law were reviewed
in 1877 in terms of pungent but righteous severity.
They had, it was said, " both the merits and defects
of English law-books in a conspicuous degree. They
represent the result of an immense quantity of patient
research and of a minutely laborious and singularly
accurate application of learning to a very unattractive
subject, but they make no pretensions to any other
merit. . . . The last edition of *Russell on Crime*
contains 2,672 closely printed royal octavo pages and
costs five and a half guineas. It is arranged in such a
manner that its last editor takes credit for having
improved it by transferring to the head of General
Provisions the title *Pleas of Autrefois Convict and
Acquit* which in the former edition appeared in the
chapter on Burglary. The first chapter having been
thus enlarged, it became advisable to decrease the
size of the first volume, and this was done by transferring the title *Bigamy and Libel* to the third volume,
where they are classed with a treatise on Evidence. . . .
The eighteenth edition of *Archbold* contains (exclusive
of the index) 1,012 very closely printed pages. I will
say nothing of the arrangement, as I suppose no one
ever paid the smallest attention to it since the book
was originally published. . . . It is an invaluable
book of reference, but to try to read it is like trying

to read a directory arranged partly on geographical and partly on biographical principles." This dissection of two respectable and domesticated books was supported by a specific stricture upon Russell's account of homicide and upon the state of the law it revealed. " Nothing short of studying the contents of these two hundred pages can give anyone any notion either of the amount of patient thought and sound good sense employed in the decision of particular cases by many generations of judges or of the immense amount of material gradually accumulated by reporters or of the hopeless bewilderment, the utter incapacity to take general views or to see the relation to each other of different principles or to arrange an intricate question according to the natural distribution of the subject which characterises English text writers. The cases, as they stand in Russell, are like the stores at Balaclava in the winter of 1854—55. Everything is there, nothing is in its place, and the few feeble attempts at arrangement which have been made serve only to bring the mass of confusion to light."

The author of this review was Sir James FitzJames Stephen; and it was he who opened a new chapter in English criminal jurisprudence.[1] He was a scion of that aristocracy of intellect which was the glory of nineteenth-century England and of which today only the shattered fragments remain. His grandfather

---

[1] The passages cited are from his *Digest of the Criminal Law*, Introduction ix–x, and pp. 365–366. The standard biography is by his brother, Leslie Stephen; but it has been enriched by the publication in 1957 of a Selden Society lecture by Dr. Leon Radzinowicz, to which is attached a bibliography and a pedigree. See also Noel Annan's *Leslie Stephen*.

devoted his years to the practice of the law, Tory politics and Evangelical philanthropy. He was the friend of Wilberforce and became a Master in Chancery. His uncle was the author of *Stephen on Pleading* and the editor of Blackstone. His father, himself a prominent Evangelical who married into the Clapham Sect, was counsel to the Colonial Office and later Under-Secretary of State. He was a man of inexhaustible, of appalling, energy. As counsel he drafted in one week-end the Bill for the abolition of the slave trade, containing 66 sections and filling 26 pages of the Statute Book; as civil servant, he was a bureaucrat of unimpeachable authority. James FitzJames Stephen was his second son and Leslie Stephen his third, and their cousin was Albert Venn Dicey. Leslie Stephen was twice married: first to Thackeray's daughter and secondly to Julia Duckworth (whose nephew was Maitland), by whom he had two daughters, Vanessa Bell and Virginia Woolf.

In 1847 FitzJames Stephen went up to Trinity College, Cambridge, where he was content to shine, in the reflected light of Maine, as an " apostle." Coming down, he read for the Bar and was adventurous enough to take the LL.B. examination of the University of London. From 1854 to 1869 he practised as a barrister; but he indulged an inordinate facility for periodical literature and achieved but moderate success in his profession. In 1869 he succeeded Maine as legal member of the Governor-General's Council in India, and, though he remained in this office for only three years, they were the most significant years of his life.

Close attention has been paid to the impact upon India of English life and English law. But the reciprocal

influence of India upon England, if less obvious, has
been persistent and fruitful. For many years before
the accession of Victoria it had been marked. In 1781
Sir William Jones, jurist and orientalist, had sought to
rationalise the law of Bailment, and his acquaintance
with Hindu law led him to examine the earlier authorities with sceptical curiosity. The exigencies of the
East India Company were constantly forcing English
lawyers to adjust their own rules to the exotic conditions
in which they had to be applied; and in the full tide
of the nineteenth century the reactions of Indian service
and environment were increasingly felt. It has been
seen that Sir Erskine Perry translated Savigny on
Possession in the hope that it would offer the Company's
aspirants and apprentices a less technical and more
worthy approach than their native law afforded to the
practical problems they had to meet.[2] Markby based
much of his *Elements of Law* upon lectures delivered
to Hindu and Mohamedan students in Calcutta.
He had tried to expound law " as a collection of
principles capable of being systematically arranged and
resting, not on bare authority, but on logical deduction." [3]
The colouring of Maine's thought and writing is palp-
able, and Pollock, in his turn, did not escape infection.
He had been instructed by the Government of India
in 1882 to prepare a Bill to codify the law of Civil
Wrongs " or so much of it as might appear to be of
practical importance in British India," and he appended
the draft to the first edition of his *Law of Torts*.

Upon Stephen the effect of Indian life and Indian

[2] *Supra*, p. 87.
[3] Preface to *Elements of Law*, 1st ed.

necessities—as experienced from the heights of auto-
cratic power—was immediate and profound. He
embraced with impatient ardour his duty and his opportunity. To legislate, and above all to codify, satisfied
an inmost urge. Inheriting as a legacy from Maine
an Indian Contract Bill, he re-drafted it and then
prepared the Indian Evidence Act. In his short time
in office he was responsible for no less than twelve
Acts and shared largely in eight others.[4]

Back in England, he resumed the double life of
law and literature.[5] He obtained considerable practice
before the Judicial Committee but otherwise made no
great mark at the Bar. In 1879 he was made a judge.
The appointment was unusual. Others, like Blackburn
and Lindley, had written books and interested themselves in jurisprudence. But, like Blackstone in the
eighteenth century, Stephen became a judge because
he was, or was thought to be, a jurist; and, as with
Blackstone, the experiment was not altogether a success.
His father's son, he was at heart a bureaucrat and,
anxious as he was to temper the law to the litigant,
he stood too far above the battle to share the litigant's
life [6] or to understand the mingled fear and irritation
of the layman caught suddenly in the strange and
intricate web of legal process. He said of himself that
he was " unteachable," and intractability is not a
judicial asset.

---

[4] See Appendix to the Lecture by Dr. Radzinowicz.

[5] Between 1865 and 1869 he contributed over 850 articles to the
Pall Mall Gazette: Radzinowicz, *op. cit.*, p. 9 and Appendix.

[6] He once shocked a Liverpool jury by asking, in all innocence,
" What is the Grand National ? " See Leslie Stephen's life
of him, pp. 96, 113.

His fame rests upon his books: *A General View of the Criminal Law of England*, *A Digest of the Criminal Law* and *A History of the Criminal Law of England*. In each he showed himself the heir of the classical English jurisprudence—of Hobbes, Bentham and Austin. Of the three Stephen was most in sympathy with Hobbes. They shared the same conservative philosophy. Both felt the need of an ordered and self-respecting society. Both were insistently aware of the swarming and degraded underworld that lay greedily awaiting the collapse of that society.[7] For Bentham he had, in his Evangelical youth, conceived a holy horror: as his early piety faltered, he came to regard him as the first and greatest of law reformers.[8] But his respect stopped well short of idolatry. He could not but feel, even as a young and not well-favoured barrister, that Bentham's contempt for the judicial office was at least exaggerated,[9] and he rejected Bentham's complacent assumptions as to the object of punishment. Retribution, in Stephen's eyes, was its primary purpose. He was simple enough to find the victim not only more deserving but more interesting than the culprit and callous enough to act on the knowledge that euphemism covers the minimum of sins. "The criminal law stands to the passion of revenge in much the same relation as marriage to the sexual appetite."[10]

Austin, as his father's friend, he had known from a child. He had felt—strange as this may now seem

---

[7] See his essay on Hobbes, reprinted in *Horae Sabbaticae*, II, 1.

[8] See the life by Leslie Stephen, 116, 207–210.

[9] *General View*, 328; *infra*, p. 134.

[10] *General View*, 98. *Cf. Hist. of Crim. Law*, II, 79–84.

to the reluctant reader of Austin's lectures—the fascination of his conversational powers. He knew, too, the
" literary " Mrs. Austin and was intrigued by their
daughter Lucy, " a brilliant girl, reputed to keep a
rifle and a skull in her bedroom." [11] For Austin as a
jurist Stephen never lost his early admiration, and
he championed him against the claims of the new
historical school asserted by Maine.[12] In his first
book he was prepared to carry Austin's premise to its
ultimate conclusion. " A law is a command enjoining
a course of conduct. A command is an intimation
from a stronger to a weaker rational being that if
the weaker does or forbears to do some specified thing
the stronger will injure or hurt him. A crime is an act
of disobedience to a law forbidden under pain of
punishment. It follows from these definitions that all
laws are in one sense criminal, for by the definitions
they must be commands and any command may be
disobeyed. . . . The notions of law and crime
are thus, in reality, correlative and co-extensive." [13]
Maturity, however, tempered the audacity of youth.
Willing disciple as he was, he was insufficiently insulated
from the business, if not from the pleasures, of life to
apply Austin's logic in all its austerity. Austin was
concerned to " determine the province of jurisprudence.''
Stephen sought to lay bare the roots of criminal liability
in order to re-make the current rules of English law.
So far, therefore, from divorcing law and morality,
he insisted on their communion. He shared the uneasy

[11] Life by Leslie Stephen, 60.
[12] *Ibid.*, 204–205, and FitzJames Stephen, "Jurisprudence" in *Horae
Sabbaticae*, II, 210.
[13] *General View*, 1–2.

conscience of the generation that succeeded Austin,
and " pure " law was to him not only impracticable
but improper.

It was true, indeed, that the moral approach to
legal problems must be scrutinised with meticulous
care. Stephen had to recognise the existence—to use a
term as helpful then and now as when employed by
Blackstone—of *mala prohibita* by the side of *mala in se.*
Already in 1863 he was aware of the " immense mass
of affairs which in other parts of the world fall under
the head of civil administration and which in this
country are transacted by the help of the criminal law ";
and in 1877 he classed them with the *contraventions*
of French law.[14] They were the teeming progeny
of convenience rather than of morality and were beneath
the attention of the criminal jurist. Morality itself
required definition. The function neither of judge nor
of jurist was to inculcate any particular code of morals.
The law " has nothing to do with truth. It is an
exclusively practical system, invented and maintained
for the purposes of an actually existing state of society.
But, though the law is entirely independent of all moral
speculation and though the judges who administer it
are, or ought to be, deaf to all arguments drawn from
such a source, it constantly refers to, and for particular
purposes notices, the moral sentiments which, as a
matter of fact, are generally entertained in the nation in
which it is established." [15] The morality of which
Stephen strove to take account was not the creed of
any church, however Erastian, and still less the inner

[14] *General View*, 5; *Digest*, Intro. vii–viii.
[15] *General View*, 90.

summons of the spirit which tempted men to uneconomic and anti-social ends and which the eighteenth century, whose views coloured his own, dismissed as "enthusiasm." It was rather the cement of a political community and, as such, an element with which the leaders of each generation must come to terms. Nor was it to be studied only in the administration of the criminal law. " The greater part of the law of contracts is an amplification of moral rules about justice and good faith." In these passages Stephen was striving, with indifferent success, to adjust the Austinian discipline to the ethical bias of the age; but he had, in truth, moved as far from Austin as from Bentham.

With these qualifications Stephen assumed criminal liability to rest upon contemporary and insular standards of morality, and he wished to simplify the English law both in substance and in form so that its credentials and its sanctions might be the more easily understood and accepted. This theme, with the variations suggested by experience, runs through his three books. *A General View of the Criminal Law of England,* published in 1863, was neither a textbook for students nor a compendium for practitioners. It was an attempt to justify criminal law as a branch of social science. Stephen challenged the attention of the good citizen in words that, in the politer or more squeamish days of Elizabeth II, would be called brutal. No part of our institutions " can have a greater moral significance or be more closely connected with broad principles of morality and politics than those by which men rightfully, deliberately and in cold blood, kill, enslave or otherwise torment their fellow creatures." For conduct to receive

and to merit such treatment, it must be promoted by a
" state of mind forbidden by the law." This state of
mind will vary according to the nature of the offence;
but it is in general denoted by the word " malice," and
malice, stripped of technical accretions, is simply
" wickedness." The detailed development of the law
may obscure this stark fact. The process of definition,
by drawing precise and therefore arbitrary lines, will
leave conduct on one side of those lines which it is
hard to distinguish from similar conduct on the other.
But to blunt the moral sensibilities is in the nature
of the legal beast. Crime remains rooted in wickedness,
and the use of the word " malice " may be defended
as " convenient " and as summarising " in a significant
way " many distinct propositions.[16]

In this book Stephen was a pioneer, and not least
on his excursions into comparative law. But, as he
came in later years to feel, and most vividly after the
discipline of directing a jury, both sentiments and
language were crude. He published his second book in
1877 after a Homicide Bill that he had drafted had
foundered in Committee. From its very loss he drew
encouragement. The main ground of rejection had
been an expressed preference for a comprehensive
Criminal Code which a particular statute was felt to
prejudice; and the Digest which he now prepared
was designed to serve as a first step towards such a
Code. Stephen had therefore to confine his text to a
strict enunciation of the existing law, though he allowed
his zeal for reform to dominate the accompanying
notes. The law of murder, he thus thought, " might

[16] *General View*, Preface and Chap. III.

be made quite reasonable " by excluding from it acts
" accompanied by an intent to commit a felony or to
resist an officer of justice in the execution of his duty." [17]
Nor was it relevant, for his present purpose, to canvass
the principles of liability. He could not, however,
resist the temptation on the one hand to correct the
youthful exuberance of his earlier book and, on the
other, to indicate the moral foundations upon which
any criminal code must rest. In his exposition of
homicide he abandoned his defence of malice as a
word of convenience and admitted its technical implications and defects. But he still thought it would
serve " as a sort of standing hint at the kind of definition
that was wanted " and would indicate the varying
degrees of " malignity " that marked the distinction
between murder and manslaughter.[18]

In 1883, when he published his most ambitious
work, *A History of the Criminal Law of England,* the
hopes that he had entertained while preparing the
Digest were finally dispelled. He had, under the
auspices of Lord Cairns, drafted a Criminal Code;
and, after a fluctuating Parliamentary career, it had
been abandoned. How far its loss is to be regretted
is a doubtful and perhaps an idle speculation. Stephen
would seem to have had many qualifications for the
task. He knew, at least, what he was about, and, like
Sir George Jessel, though he might be wrong, he never
doubted. He saw no reason why an Act of Parliament
should not be well written. " The subject must be
dull, but the style may be lively. Each word may

---

[17] *Digest of the Criminal Law,* Introduction, xxxvii.
[18] *Ibid.,* 359.

add to the sense and may be put in the right place,
whether the subject in hand is Paradise Lost or the
Statute of Frauds." [19] He could call upon his own
Indian experiences and the example of Macaulay. But
it is a sad reflection upon the irony of human ambition
that the Indian legislation of which he was so proud
has not escaped criticism. Lord Bryce said of him
that " his capacity for the work of drafting was not
equal to his fondness for it." Pollock described his
share of the Indian Contract Act as a " source of
unequal workmanship and sometimes of positive error."
Sir Courtenay Ilbert called him " a Cyclopean builder.
He hurled together huge blocks of rough-hewn law . . .
and left behind him in the Indian Statute Book some
defective courses of masonry which his successors had
to remove and replace." [20] If, as Stephen himself
declared, " an ideal code ought to be drawn by a Bacon
and settled by a Coke," [21] it is easy to understand why
it remains an ideal.

It was thus in all the disappointment of a ruling
passion that Stephen turned to the history of the
criminal law. It caught him, so to speak, on the rebound.
He confessed in the preface the surprise with which he
discovered that history could be interesting. His
approach, indeed, was that of an unenthusiastic amateur.
Though the new methods of historical scholarship had
already permeated the law and Maitland was revealing

[19] *Digest of the Criminal Law*, Introduction, xx–xxii.
[20] Bryce, *Studies in History and Jurisprudence*, I, 128–130; Pollock
and Mulla, *Indian Contract Act*, Preface to 1st ed.; Ilbert,
10 L.Q.R. 222. It is fair to add that Dr. Radzinowicz puts a
higher value on Stephen's work as a draftsman. See his Selden
Society Lecture, 13–22.
[21] *History of the Criminal Law*, III, 300.

its possibilities, Stephen was but an historian *malgré lui*. He was not interested in the past and he could not think himself back beyond the eighteenth century. The book is fascinating; but its fascination lies in the revelation, not of the growth of the law, but of the author's own elemental character. It is a self-portrait of unconscious fidelity, warts and all. It remains a testament to his faith in a criminal law based broadly upon popular morality. As he surveyed the England of 1883, institutional religion was a waning force and the attempt to replace it by humanitarianism, as his own brother had found, pitifully inadequate. Only the law remained. If he could not base life upon faith, he must support it by works—or at least by fear. In the rhetorical close to the *History* he rehearsed his creed. " The criminal law may be described with truth as an expansion of the second table of the Ten Command-ments. The statement in the Catechism of the positive duties of man to man corresponds step by step with the prohibitions of a Criminal Code." The time was ripe to " preach such a sermon in the most emphatic tones. . . . The religious sanction has been immensely weakened, and unlimited licence to every one to think as he pleases on all subjects, and especially on moral and religious subjects, is leading many people to the conclusion that if they do not happen to like morality there is no reason why they should be moral. In such circumstances it seems to be specially necessary for those who do care for morality to make its one un-questionable, indisputable sanction as clear and strong and emphatic as words and act can make it. A man may disbelieve in God, heaven and hell, he may care little for mankind or society or for the nation to which he belongs—let him at least be plainly told what are the acts that will stamp him with infamy, hold him up to public execration and bring him to the gallows, the gaol or the lash." [22]

With this vigorous peroration Stephen closed not only his own but all substantial Victorian contributions to criminal jurisprudence in England. There had, indeed, been published at Cambridge in 1880 a slim volume from the unlikely pen of the Regius Professor of Civil Law.[23] Professor Clark's *Analysis of Criminal Liability* was founded on Austin as interpreted by Stephen. The author shared the views and prejudices of both his mentors. He expected the early advent of a code, and he looked forward to the time when legal rules might be stated with the precision of mathematics and when criminal law would " receive little, if any, additions from later cases because a new point could scarcely arise." The book seems to have had no influence when it appeared and it has had none since. To examine it further would be an exercise in morbid pathology.

In Boston, however, Holmes read the *History of the Criminal Law* in the year of its publication. He did not think much of it. Stephen, he wrote to Pollock, was " an adult male animal, but he hasn't the intuition of Maine or the higher class of writers." [24] Holmes had already expressed his own views in his lectures on the Common Law. Criminal liability, in the infancy of

[22] *History of the Criminal Law*, III, 366–367.
[23] E. C. Clark, *An Analysis of Criminal Liability*. Kenny's *Outlines of Criminal Law* was not published until 1902.
[24] *Pollock–Holmes Letters*, I, 21.

society, had its roots in revenge and its pattern in morality. But, whereas to Stephen it was still the embodiment of ethics, to Holmes legal alchemy was always transmuting moral ideas into a metal of less clumsy if not baser character. In the nineteenth century the test of criminality should be the degree of danger shown in practice to attach to any particular conduct. The obliquity of the individual was irrelevant. " The reference to the prudent man, as a standard, is the only form in which blameworthiness, as such, is an element of crime." [25] The moral criterion was the relic of an untutored age, social or political expediency the sole test, and the history of the criminal law a branch of evolutionary or biological science.

Holmes here drew the inexorable conclusion of his legal syllogism. It is arguable that civil liability is not based on fault, and it is indeed doubtful if it may be explained in terms of any single principle. But, in applying the same analysis to criminal liability, Holmes would seem to have forgotten his own aphorism that experience and not logic is the life of the law.[26] If Stephen too vehemently pressed the claims of a criminal code as a Victorian substitute for the Decalogue, Holmes ignored too disdainfully the sentiments of the unsophisticated citizen upon whose passive acquiescence the authority of any law ultimately depends. It would be portentous and unmeaning to say of his thesis that it " shocks the conscience of mankind." But it certainly affronts the instincts of ordinary people, and it is their

---

[25] *The Common Law*, 37–38: 75–76.
[26] He remembered it in other passages of his lecture on the Criminal Law, *e.g.*, *The Common Law*, 41.

expectations that the machinery of the courts is designed to implement.

The English judges, at least, had they been required to make their election, would have chosen to follow Stephen rather than Holmes. In tort their response to the equation of fault and liability was fitful and unconvincing; but in the criminal law they received it as axiomatic. There were some who, as they showed in their gyrations around the problem of Possession,[27] went so far as to think it their duty to convict a dishonest man even if this demanded a strained and artificial construction of technical rules. But even if this was to others too positive a recognition of moral claims, all accepted the negative assumption that no man should be punished by the common law who was not, as Stephen had insisted, in some manner or degree a " wicked " man.

It was because they assumed without demur the ethical basis of criminal liability that the judges sought to delimit the frontiers of crime and tort. The boundaries could not be traced with certitude or finality, but they had no doubt of the principles upon which the task should be attempted. Negligent conduct, for instance, might merit punishment as well as invite compensation, and the grades of carelessness were scarcely susceptible of actuarial calculation. But Mr. Justice Willes expressed the general view when, on an indictment for manslaughter against a doctor whose patient had died from an overdose of strychnine, he told the jury that " if they thought the prosecution had made out a case in which the circumstances showed

[27] *Supra*, p. 104.

such gross and culpable negligence as would amount to a culpable wrong and show an evil mind, they ought to convict the prisoner, and, if not, they ought to acquit." [28] The language is neither elegant nor precise. But Willes was not composing a judgment, he was directing a jury; and at assizes or quarter sessions refinements are out of place. It was his duty to offer a measure of guilt which, if rough, the jury might at least find ready and, if they thought fit, apply. If the supply of vituperative epithets ran dry, recourse might be had to tautology: negligence should be a crime if it could be described as criminal. Upon the same assumption and for the same reasons the doctrine of vicarious liability, convenient if not necessary in the law of torts, had no place in the common law of crime. It followed that a corporation, which might by this device be required to pay compensation, could not with propriety be punished as a criminal. In *R.* v. *Great North of England Ry.*[29] Lord Denman admitted the existence of administrative regulations, masquerading as crimes, which corporations no less than human beings must observe or pay forfeit. But no indictment for felony would lie. Serious offences, he said, " plainly derive their character from the corrupted mind of the person committing them and are violations of the social duties that belong to men and subjects. A corporation, which has no such duties, cannot be guilty in such cases."

The shibboleth of the common law was the phrase *Actus non facit reum nisi mens sit rea.* Stephen examined

[28] *R.* v. *Spencer* (1867) 10 Cox 525. The jury acquitted.
[29] (1846) 9 Q.B. 315.

it in an interesting chapter of his *History*.[30] With unusual playfulness he termed it not so much a maxim as a minim. It was dark in origin, doubtful in meaning, dangerous in implication. Not only did it lead the unwary student to confuse intent and motive, but it suggested a single state of mind as essential to all crimes. In reality the common law recognised differing states of mind appropriate to different offences, and each must be defined before *mens rea* could be evaluated. Yet, with all these qualifications, it pointed the vital truth that, before an Englishman was to be treated as a criminal, some mental deformity, some taint of evil, must accompany his physical acts.

Tendentious or misleading, the phrase was always on judicial lips. It was, said Chief Justice Cockburn, " the foundation of all criminal justice." [31] Nor was it to be confined to the common law. As the long reign wore on, ever more statutes crowded upon the Queen's judges. But they sought to isolate those which properly imposed criminal liability from those which were the mere tools of government, and even in the latter they were slow to believe that Parliament was prepared to sacrifice ethics to expediency. For their part they would not lightly countenance so cynical a course. Lord Campbell, that tough insensitive Scot, did not readily succumb to sentiment; yet even he failed to escape the moral contagion. In 1856 he dismissed a charge against a defendant who had inadvertently broken a statute,[32] and in 1859 he upheld

---

[30] Vol. II, Chap. XVIII.

[31] *R.* v. *Sheep* (1861) 8 Cox 472.

[32] *Bowman* v. *Blyth* (1856) 7 E. & B. 26. In this very year Lord Campbell was described by Stephen: " He was thickset as a

justices in a refusal to convict consignors who had sent for carriage a quantity of " oil of vitriol " without notifying the nature of the goods as required by statute. The consignors had reasonably believed that the goods were adequately marked. " The justices," said Lord Campbell, " were perfectly right: *actus non facit reum nisi mens sit rea.* The act with which the respondents were charged is an offence created by statute and for which the person committing it is liable to a penalty or to imprisonment. . . . There was neither negligence nor moral guilt of any kind on their part." [33] Two years later Chief Justice Cockburn candidly avowed the predominant influence of the common law. " The ordinary principle that there must be a guilty mind to constitute a guilty act must be imported into this statute." [34]

Despite this declaration of independence it was not always easy for a judge to bend a stubborn statute to his purpose. The problem of interpretation is one of the most exasperating that litigants can offer. It is not indeed confined to the law. Its roots lie deep in the intricacies of language, and it is but one aspect of the wider problem of communicating thought. To the theologian it is a perennial stumbling-block. In the

navvy, as hard as nails, still full of vigour at the age of 76 and looking fit for ten or twelve more years of work " (*Life* by Leslie Stephen, 140).

[33] *Hearne* v. *Gorton* (1859) 2 E. & E. 66.
[34] *R.* v. *Sheep* (1861) 8 Cox 472. The defendant was charged under a statute of William III with being in possession of naval stores marked with the broad arrow. On the finding of the jury that there was no sufficient evidence to show that the defendant knew they were so marked, it was ruled that he could not be convicted, despite the peremptory language of the statute.

words of Alexander Hamilton,[35] " when the Almighty himself condescends to address mankind in their own language, His meaning, luminous as it must be, is rendered dim by the cloudy medium through which it is communicated." In temporal affairs it is met by everybody: the secretary when he writes a minute, the business man when he makes notes of a contract, the lawyer when he settles an estate or drafts a will. It is not surprising that a process at once so common and so complex should have intrigued philosophers and even psychologists and that a textbook on *The Meaning of Meaning* should have passed through ten editions.[36]

A statute, the most ambitious of documents, is also the most equivocal. In the first half of the nineteenth century the judges evolved three rules which, it was hoped, might aid them in their task.[37] By the Literal Rule, if the words of a statute were plain, the courts must apply them, whatever the consequences. *Fiat littera, ruant litigatores.* By the Golden Rule, sponsored by Baron Parke, plain though the words might be, the judges could depart from them if they would otherwise be led into absurdity or manifest injustice, or if the result would upset the balance of the statute as a whole. By the Mischief Rule, if the words were ambiguous, they might be widened or restricted according to the judicial view of legislative policy. Superficially simple, the rules contained the seeds of confusion. The first two were to be used as alternatives

[35] *The Federalist*, No. 36.
[36] *The Meaning of Meaning*: Ogden and Richards.
[37] See Willis, *Statutory Interpretation in a Nutshell*, 16 Can. Bar.Rev. 1.

when the meaning was plain; the third when it was doubtful. But this very assumption, that any given collection of words, statutory or otherwise, possesses a single, predetermined, invariable meaning, begs the whole question. It is precisely the absence of any such immutable quality that provokes and confuses the process of interpretation. As Holmes reminded his generation, " a word generally has several meanings even in the dictionary." [38] More than one case can be cited where the members of a court agreed that the meaning of a section was plain, but differed as to what that plain meaning might be.[39] A lively mind, more-over, could always detect a convenient ambiguity, and in practice judges chose the particular rule that policy or temperament indicated.[40]

The judicial attitude is sufficiently shown by the well-known cases of *R.* v. *Prince* and *R.* v. *Tolson*.[41] Each was a set piece staged before the Court for Crown Cases Reserved. Prince was indicted under an Act of 1861 for unlawfully taking an unmarried girl under the age of sixteen out of the possession and against the will of her father. His belief on good grounds that she was over that age was held to be no defence and he was convicted. The conviction was sustained by fourteen judges, though only two substantial judgments were delivered. Mr. Justice Blackburn applied the Literal Rule. The statutory

---

[38] *Theory of Legal Interpretation*, Coll. Papers, 203.

[39] For a modern example, see *Ellerman Lines* v. *Murray* [1931] A.C. 126.

[40] *e.g.*, *Gwynne* v. *Burnell* (1840) 6 Bing.N.C. 453.

[41] *R.* v. *Prince* (1875) L.R. 2 C.C.R. 154; *R.* v. *Tolson* (1889) 23 Q.B.D. 168.

prohibition was plain, it would lead to no absurdity
or injustice, and to import common law presumptions
was neither necessary nor desirable. Baron Bramwell,
while he concurred in the result, was less circumspect.
He had condemned the tendency to stretch the law of
larceny in order to make the dishonest man a criminal.[42]
He was equally determined not to allow honest or
neutral conduct to be converted into a crime by the
mere words of an Act. They must be read so as to fit
the doctrine of *mens rea*. On the facts of the case
the doctrine was fortunately satisfied: the defendant's
conduct, apart from the statute, was morally wrong,
and he must pay the penalty. In *R.* v. *Tolson* the
defendant was indicted for bigamy under another
section of the same Act. She had gone through the
ceremony of marriage with another man five years
after her husband had deserted her and in the honest
and reasonable belief that he was dead. The only
relevant defence expressed in the Act was absence
" for the space of seven years." The defendant was
tried before Mr. Justice Stephen at the Carlisle Assizes.
He summed up for a conviction, secured it, sentenced
the defendant to one day's imprisonment and reserved
the case to be considered by his brethren. By a majority
of nine to five the conviction was quashed. Stephen
himself, who had hoped for this conclusion, took the
opportunity to restate his views on *mens rea*. Treacher-
ous as it was, the phrase at least required " the full
definition of every crime to contain expressly or by
implication a proposition as to a state of mind." The
requirement could be excluded by the words of a statute,

[42] *Supra*, p. 104.

but only by language free from ambiguity. In the present case there was no such language, and policy suggested that common law principles should prevail. Mr. Justice Cave agreed. Parliament was doubtless omnipotent and could, if it would, make innocence criminal. " But such a result seems so revolting to the moral sense that we ought to demand the clearest and most indisputable evidence that such is the meaning of the Act." Mr. Justice Wills contrasted the case with that of *R*. v. *Prince*. Individual statutes and sections must be individually construed in the light both of common law and of common sense. The defendant in the earlier case had been guilty of conduct which all good men must deplore: here neither the defendant's actions nor the words of the section excluded the hypothesis that " there can be no crime without a tainted mind." The suspicion is strong that in neither case would the interpretation have been the same had Henry Prince not been a cad and Martha Tolson not more sinned against than sinning.

Set against the sophistication of twentieth-century scholarship, Stephen's essays in jurisprudence and the judicial reactions to the practical problems of the criminal law may seem ingenuous and incomplete. They lacked coherence and left unsettled such central issues as the definition of murder. But they reflected faithfully the contemporary egoism that sought neither the fraternal discipline of the police state nor the *diablerie* of the psychiatrist. The citizen felt that the judge met him as man to man and that the justice administered to and for him conformed to his social and ethical standards.

Chapter 6

CONCLUSION

The scattered problems desultorily discussed in these lectures—the basis of civil and of criminal liability, the nature of corporations, the mysteries of possession —may serve to show, if demonstration be needed, that judge and jurist approach the law from different angles and with differing aims. The judge is a law-maker. In his first book Stephen dismissed as childishly transparent the fiction by which it has sometimes been sought to conceal this fact, and offered a tribute as deserved as it was discriminating. " The English judges have always formed one of the best subordinate legislatures in the world. They are the picked members of the most active and energetic profession in the country, by the members of which their decisions are jealously tested and criticised. . . . They are numerous enough to give their decisions weight, but not enough to lose their individual sense of responsibility." [1] But the law thus made is the by-product of a more intimate process, the administration of justice—almost an accident arising out of and in the course of the judicial employment. Like liberty and equality, law and justice are barely compatible, and all that may be entreated is a tolerable compromise. The judge must formulate his principle within the pattern imposed by the chance medley of litigation, and he knows the

[1] Stephen, *General View*, 328.

134

danger of a premature synthesis. To generalise at large is perilous. Striking exceptions exist as Willes and Blackburn proved, creative minds in a creative age. But for the most part the generalisation must be tentative and accommodating. To follow an argument to its logical conclusion is to invite absurdity. The judge must be guided by what Newman called the " illative sense "; he must rely not so much on ratiocination as on an instinct cultivated by long experience in a close corporation of minds.

This very instinct and this very communion may, indeed, lead the judges into an impasse. They may adhere too obstinately to a decision, given perhaps hastily in the first instance or encrusted with minute distinctions or now out of touch with daily needs. Legal thought may have stiffened into phrases and the phrases become themselves objects of reverence, to be venerated, as Blackstone said of the English Constitution, where it is not possible presently to comprehend. Sometimes a bold and dominant personality like Macnaghten may strike through the tangle at a blow. More often it is necessary to change the climate of professional opinion. It is here that the jurist can help, by retracing the judicial steps, by detecting the *raison d'être* of the original decision and discovering both its current ineptitude and the way of escape from the tyranny of dogma. He can be a valuable instrument of reform, provided that he remembers that " if it is not necessary to change, it is necessary not to change."

The jurist has a second function. If the judge sees the law steadily, he cannot see it whole. It is for the jurist, at long range, to co-ordinate the immediate answers to fortuitous problems. In the very detachment which this task demands lie insidious temptations. To systematise is to simplify: to simplify is to distort. The complexity of the law reflects the chaos of life. It may or may not be possible to devise an English tragedy according to the classical doctrine of the unities: the vision of an English jurisprudence so constructed is grotesque. The jurist, moreover, while he should be dispassionate, must not cease to be human. Henry James saw his characters as " jolly little things dancing under the writing lamp." [2] While the most hardened judge may not dare so to think of the litigant, it is fatally easy for the jurist to accept him as the material—only too raw—of his legal equations.

Though their opportunities and temptations thus diverge, judge and jurist are nevertheless complementary craftsmen. Together they can make law that is rooted in principle and yet pliant in the handling, at once tough and flexible. But, save for Austin, English jurisprudence flowered too late to be a formative influence of major importance in the lives of Victoria's judges. Their successors were bred in a different school; and, if one figure may serve as a link between the generations, it is that of Pollock.[3] Equally at home in the Inns of Court and in the Universities, he was for sixty years at the heart of the law. A brooding presence near the Bench, he might have supplied the answer to the question, *Quis custodiet ipsos custodes*? Rooted in the virtues that have come, with whatever truth, to be called Victorian, the fruits of his scholarship

---

[2] Said by James to Quiller-Couch: *Fifty Years 1882–1932*, p. 53.
[3] As in the United States, it is that of Holmes.

were harvested by men who were themselves the products of a new legal education. That story is outside the scope of these lectures. To recall the judges and jurists of the nineteenth century may provide an antidote to the most vulgar and provincial of modern heresies—the indifference or contempt for any age but one's own, the impudent assumption that the world belongs to the living and is a property in which the dead hold no shares. At least the lawyers of Victoria, on the Bench or in the study, left us an example and a heritage. We can do worse than follow the one and cultivate what remains of the other.

INDEX